Breaking the Mold: A Young Person's Guide to Entrepreneurship

Maja Nice

Table Of Contents

Chapter 1: Introduction to Entrepreneurship

What is Entrepreneurship?

Entrepreneurship is a term that is often thrown around, but what does it really mean? In simple terms, entrepreneurship is the process of identifying, creating, and pursuing opportunities to start and grow a business. It is about taking risks, being innovative, and having the drive to turn ideas into reality.

For young people interested in becoming entrepreneurs, the journey begins with a passion or a problem they want to solve. It could be a product or service they believe in or a social issue they are passionate about. Entrepreneurship allows them to channel their energy and creativity into making a difference in the world.

To become an entrepreneur, there are certain qualities and skills that one needs to develop. Firstly, it is important to have a strong work ethic and perseverance. Starting a business is not easy, and there will be challenges along the way. Being able to stay focused and committed to the vision is crucial.

Secondly, entrepreneurs need to be adaptable and open to learning. The business landscape is constantly evolving, and it is important to stay updated with the latest trends and technologies. Continuous learning and seeking out new knowledge will help entrepreneurs stay ahead of the game.

For those interested in becoming a social media entrepreneur, the key lies in understanding the power of social media platforms. Social media has become a powerful tool for marketing and reaching a wide audience. By leveraging these platforms effectively, young entrepreneurs can build and grow their businesses.

Similarly, for those interested in becoming sustainable entrepreneurs, the focus is on creating businesses that have a positive impact on the environment and society. Sustainable entrepreneurs find innovative ways to address environmental challenges while still making a profit. They aim to create a business model that is both socially and environmentally responsible.

In conclusion, entrepreneurship is about taking risks, following one's passion, and making a difference. Whether you want to become a traditional entrepreneur, a social media entrepreneur, or a sustainable entrepreneur, the key is to believe in yourself and your ideas. With hard work, perseverance, and a willingness to learn, young people have the power to break the mold and create their own path in the world of entrepreneurship.

Why Should You Consider Becoming an Entrepreneur?

In today's rapidly changing world, the traditional career path is no longer the only option for young people. The rise of entrepreneurship has opened up a whole new world of possibilities and opportunities. Becoming an entrepreneur can bring immense fulfilment, personal growth, and financial independence. In this subchapter, we will explore why you should seriously consider becoming an entrepreneur and how it can transform your life.

First and foremost, becoming an entrepreneur allows you to be your own boss. You have the freedom to set your own schedule, choose your projects, and pursue your passions. Instead of working for someone else and following someone else's vision, you get to build and shape your own future. This autonomy and control over your destiny can be incredibly empowering and satisfying.

Entrepreneurship also offers limitless potential for personal growth. As an entrepreneur, you are constantly faced with new challenges and obstacles to overcome. This requires you to continuously learn, adapt, and develop new skills. Whether it's honing your leadership abilities, mastering marketing strategies, or sharpening your problem-solving skills, the journey of entrepreneurship is a continuous learning experience that pushes you to your limits and helps you grow as an individual.

Moreover, becoming an entrepreneur allows you to make a positive impact on the world. With the rise of social media and sustainable practices, there are now niches within entrepreneurship that focus on making a difference. If you are passionate about social causes or environmental sustainability, you can use entrepreneurship as a platform to create meaningful change. Becoming a social media entrepreneur or a sustainable entrepreneur allows you to combine your passions with business, enabling you to create a positive impact on society while pursuing your dreams.

Lastly, entrepreneurship offers the potential for financial independence and wealth creation. While success is not guaranteed, the ability to create your own business and control your financial destiny is unparalleled. As an entrepreneur, you have the opportunity to build a profitable business that generates income and creates wealth. This financial freedom can provide you with the resources and flexibility to live life on your own terms and pursue your dreams without limitations.

In conclusion, becoming an entrepreneur opens up a world of possibilities and opportunities for young people. It offers autonomy, personal growth, the chance to make a positive impact, and the potential for financial independence. Whether you aspire to become a general entrepreneur or specialize in social media or sustainable entrepreneurship, embarking on the entrepreneurial journey can be a life-changing experience. So, dare to break the mold and consider becoming an entrepreneur. Your future is waiting to be transformed.

The Benefits and Challenges of Entrepreneurship

In today's fast-paced and ever-evolving world, entrepreneurship has become an attractive career path for young people. Breaking the Mold: A Young Person's Guide to Entrepreneurship explores the benefits and challenges that come with embarking on this exciting journey. Whether you aspire to become a traditional entrepreneur, a social media entrepreneur, or a sustainable entrepreneur, this subchapter provides valuable insights to help you navigate the path to success.

Entrepreneurship offers numerous benefits that can shape your personal and professional life. One of the key advantages is the opportunity to be your own boss. As an entrepreneur, you have the freedom to make decisions, set your own schedule, and pursue your passion. This autonomy fosters creativity and allows you to build a business aligned with your values and interests. Moreover, entrepreneurship opens doors to financial independence and unlimited earning potential. By creating innovative products or services, you can generate substantial profits and secure your financial future.

However, entrepreneurship also comes with its fair share of challenges. Starting a business requires dedication, perseverance, and a strong work ethic. You must be willing to take risks and step out of your comfort zone. Failure is an inevitable part of the entrepreneurial journey, but it should be seen as a learning opportunity rather than a setback. Embracing failure helps you grow, learn from your mistakes, and ultimately achieve success.

For those interested in becoming a social media entrepreneur, this subchapter delves into the unique aspects of this niche. In today's digital age, social media platforms have become powerful tools for business growth. By leveraging your creativity and digital skills, you can build an online presence, engage with your target audience, and monetize your content. This subchapter provides practical tips on choosing the right platform, creating compelling content, and growing your online community.

Furthermore, with the increasing focus on sustainability and environmental consciousness, becoming a sustainable entrepreneur has gained prominence. This subchapter explores how you can build a business that not only generates profits but also has a positive impact on the planet. From incorporating eco-friendly practices into your operations to creating sustainable products or services, you can contribute to a greener future while running a successful business.

In conclusion, the benefits of entrepreneurship are diverse and enticing, but it's important to acknowledge the challenges that come along with it. Breaking the Mold: A Young Person's Guide to Entrepreneurship empowers you with the knowledge, tools, and inspiration to embark on your entrepreneurial journey, whether you choose to become a traditional, social media, or sustainable entrepreneur. By understanding the benefits and challenges, you can navigate the path to success and create a fulfilling and impactful career.

Chapter 2: How to Become an Entrepreneur

Identifying Your Passion and Skills

In the journey towards becoming an entrepreneur, one of the most crucial steps is to identify your passion and skills. This subchapter will guide young people aspiring to become entrepreneurs, particularly those interested in the niches of becoming a general entrepreneur, a social media entrepreneur, or a sustainable entrepreneur.

Passion is the driving force that fuels entrepreneurs' determination and commitment to their ventures. It is essential to identify what truly excites and motivates you. Take some time for self-reflection and ask yourself a few fundamental questions: What are your interests? What topics or activities energize you? What problems do you feel inspired to solve? By pinpointing your passion, you can align your entrepreneurial journey with the things that truly matter to you.

Next, take inventory of your skills and strengths. Identify the unique abilities and knowledge you possess that can contribute to your entrepreneurial success. Are you a great communicator? Do you have a knack for problem-solving? Are you adept at utilizing social media platforms? Recognizing and leveraging your skills will help you find your niche and excel in your chosen field.

For those interested in becoming a social media entrepreneur, it is crucial to have a deep understanding of various social media platforms and their functionalities. Develop your skills in content creation, community management, and digital marketing to establish a strong online presence. Learn to analyze trends, engage with your audience, and create captivating content that resonates with your target market.

If your passion lies in becoming a sustainable entrepreneur, focus on developing an understanding of environmental and social issues. Familiarize yourself with sustainable practices and innovative solutions that can address these challenges. Build a network of like-minded individuals and organizations, and seek out mentorship opportunities from professionals in the field.

Remember, identifying your passion and skills is an ongoing process. As you grow and evolve, your interests and abilities may change. Embrace this evolution and continuously seek opportunities to learn and develop new skills.

In conclusion, becoming an entrepreneur requires identifying your passion and skills. By aligning your entrepreneurial journey with your interests and leveraging your unique abilities, you can set yourself up for success. Whether you aspire to become a general entrepreneur, a social media entrepreneur, or a sustainable entrepreneur, discovering and nurturing your passion and skills will be the foundation for a fulfilling and successful entrepreneurial career.

Researching and Validating Your Business Idea

When it comes to starting your own business, having a great idea is just the beginning. It's crucial to thoroughly research and validate your business idea before diving into the world of entrepreneurship. This subchapter will guide young people interested in becoming entrepreneurs, particularly those interested in social media and sustainable entrepreneurship, on how to effectively research and validate their business ideas.

First, start by identifying your target market. Who are your potential customers? What are their needs and pain points? Conduct surveys, interviews, and focus groups to gather valuable insights and understand their preferences. This will help you tailor your product or service to meet their demands.

Next, analyze your competition. Understanding the competitive landscape is essential for success. Research similar businesses and identify their strengths and weaknesses. This will help you differentiate your offering and find a unique selling proposition that sets you apart.

Additionally, conduct a thorough market analysis. Study industry trends, market size, and growth potential. Are there any existing gaps in the market that your business can fill? By understanding the market dynamics, you can position your business for success.

Once you have gathered sufficient data, it's time to validate your business idea. Start by creating a minimum viable product (MVP) or prototype to test with your target audience. Seek feedback and iterate based on their suggestions. This iterative process will enable you to refine your idea and ensure its viability.

Furthermore, consider the financial aspect of your business. Conduct a feasibility study to determine the financial feasibility and potential profitability of your idea. Create a budget, project your revenues and expenses, and assess your break-even point. This will give you a clear understanding of the financial viability of your business.

Lastly, it's important to seek advice and mentorship from experienced entrepreneurs in your chosen niche. Join entrepreneurship communities, attend networking events, and reach out to industry experts for guidance. Their insights and experiences can provide invaluable guidance and help you avoid common pitfalls.

Remember, entrepreneurship requires meticulous research and validation. By thoroughly researching your target market, competition, and industry, and validating your business idea through prototypes and feedback, you are setting yourself up for success as a young entrepreneur. Whether you aspire to be a social media entrepreneur or a sustainable entrepreneur, these steps will lay a strong foundation for your entrepreneurial journey.

Creating a Business Plan

Securing Funding and Resources

One of the most crucial aspects of starting any business venture is securing funding and resources. Whether you aspire to become a traditional entrepreneur, a social media entrepreneur, or a sustainable entrepreneur, understanding how to secure the necessary resources is essential for your success. In this subchapter, we will explore various strategies and tips to help you navigate the world of funding and resources.

First and foremost, it is important to have a clear vision and a well-defined business plan. Whether you are starting a tech startup or a non-profit organization, having a solid plan in place will make it easier to convince potential investors or sponsors to support your venture. Your business plan should outline your goals, target audience, revenue streams, and marketing strategies. It should also highlight the potential social or environmental impact your business aims to achieve.

When it comes to funding, there are several options you can consider. Traditional methods include seeking loans from banks or applying for grants from government or private institutions. However, in recent years, alternative funding sources such as crowdfunding platforms have gained popularity, especially for young entrepreneurs. These platforms allow you to pitch your idea to a wide audience and attract individual donors who believe in your vision.

For social media entrepreneurs, building a strong online presence is key. By leveraging social media platforms such as Instagram, YouTube, or TikTok, you can reach a large audience and attract potential sponsors or advertisers. It is essential to create engaging and authentic content that resonates with your target audience. Collaborating with other influencers or brands in your niche can also open doors to additional funding opportunities.

Sustainable entrepreneurs face a unique challenge as they strive to balance profitability with positive environmental or social impact. To secure funding, it is important to identify investors or organizations that are aligned with your values and mission. Many impact investors or sustainable development funds specifically seek out businesses that prioritize sustainability. Networking and attending conferences or events focused on sustainability can help you connect with potential partners or investors who share your vision.

In conclusion, securing funding and resources is a crucial step in becoming a successful entrepreneur, regardless of your chosen niche. By developing a strong business plan, exploring various funding options, and leveraging the power of social media or sustainability networks, you can increase your chances of obtaining the necessary resources to turn your entrepreneurial dreams into reality. Remember, perseverance, passion, and a solid plan are the keys to unlocking the doors of funding and resources.

Setting Up Your Business

Starting your own business can be an exciting and rewarding journey, offering you the opportunity to pursue your passions, make an impact, and become your own boss. Whether you aspire to be a traditional entrepreneur, a social media entrepreneur, or a sustainable entrepreneur, this subchapter will guide you through the essential steps of setting up your business.

1. Define Your Vision: Before diving into the details, it's crucial to have a clear vision for your business. What problem are you solving? What values will your business uphold? Take time to brainstorm and outline your mission statement, as this will serve as the foundation for your entire business.

2. Conduct Market Research: Understanding your target audience and the market you're entering is vital. Identify your potential customers, analyze your competitors, and study industry trends. This research will help you tailor your products or services to meet the needs and preferences of your target market.

3. Develop a Business Plan: A well-crafted business plan will outline your goals, strategies, financial projections, and marketing tactics. It will serve as a roadmap for your business's success and can be used to attract investors or secure funding. Take time to research and write a comprehensive business plan that will guide you through the initial stages and future growth of your venture.

4. Set Up Legal and Financial Structures: Register your business with the appropriate authorities, such as obtaining a business license or incorporating your company. Consult with legal and financial professionals to ensure compliance with regulations and establish the right financial structures, such as opening a business bank account and setting up bookkeeping systems.

5. Build Your Brand: Your brand is more than just a logo. It encompasses your values, personality, and the way you communicate with your audience. Create a compelling brand identity that resonates with your target market and reflects your business's unique selling proposition. Develop a strong online presence through social media platforms relevant to your niche.

6. Implement Marketing Strategies: Effective marketing will help you reach your target audience and generate sales. Leverage social media and digital marketing techniques tailored to your specific business niche. Utilize content marketing, influencer collaborations, and search engine optimization to increase your brand visibility and attract customers.

7. Embrace Sustainability: If you aspire to be a sustainable entrepreneur, incorporate eco-friendly practices into your business operations. Reduce waste, source sustainable materials, and promote ethical production practices. Communicate your commitment to sustainability, as it can attract like-minded customers and provide a competitive edge.

Remember, entrepreneurship is a journey, and it requires dedication, perseverance, and continuous learning. Surround yourself with mentors, network with other entrepreneurs, and stay updated on industry trends. By following these steps and staying true to your vision, you can break the mold and build a successful business that aligns with your passions and values.

Developing a Marketing Strategy

In today's fast-paced and highly competitive business world, developing a solid marketing strategy is crucial for the success of any entrepreneurial venture. Whether you aspire to become a traditional entrepreneur, a social media entrepreneur, or a sustainable entrepreneur, understanding the importance of marketing and how to effectively implement it can make all the difference.

To begin, let's clarify what a marketing strategy entails. Simply put, it is a plan that outlines how you will promote and sell your products or services to your target audience. It involves identifying your target market, understanding their needs and preferences, and crafting a message that resonates with them. A well-developed marketing strategy will help you connect with your customers, build brand awareness, and ultimately drive sales.

When it comes to becoming an entrepreneur, your marketing strategy acts as the backbone of your business. It helps you differentiate yourself from competitors, attract customers, and establish your brand identity. For young entrepreneurs, it is essential to leverage the power of technology and social media. By understanding the ins and outs of social media marketing, you can tap into the vast online community to promote your products or services effectively.

For those interested in becoming a social media entrepreneur, your marketing strategy should revolve around building a strong online presence, engaging with your target audience, and creating compelling content. Social media platforms provide an excellent opportunity to connect with potential customers, gather feedback, and create a loyal following. By understanding the algorithms and trends of popular social media platforms, you can effectively market your products or services and build a thriving online business.

Moreover, sustainability has become a key concern for many young entrepreneurs. As a sustainable entrepreneur, your marketing strategy should focus on highlighting the environmentally-friendly aspects of your business. By promoting your sustainable practices and values, you can attract like-minded customers who prioritize eco-friendly products or services. Utilizing digital marketing tools and platforms can help you reach a wider audience and educate them about the importance of sustainable living.

In conclusion, developing a marketing strategy is an essential step for any aspiring entrepreneur. Whether you aim to become a traditional entrepreneur, a social media entrepreneur, or a sustainable entrepreneur, understanding the fundamentals of marketing is crucial. By identifying your target market, crafting a compelling message, and leveraging technology and social media, you can effectively promote your products or services and create a successful business venture. Embrace the power of marketing, and you'll be one step closer to achieving your entrepreneurial dreams.

Managing Finances and Operations

In today's fast-paced, ever-changing world, entrepreneurship has become an increasingly popular career path for young people. Whether you dream of starting your own business, becoming a social media influencer, or making a positive impact on the environment as a sustainable entrepreneur, managing your finances and operations effectively is crucial to your success. In this subchapter, we will explore essential principles and strategies to help you navigate the complex world of entrepreneurship.

Financial management is the backbone of any successful venture. Aspiring entrepreneurs must develop a strong understanding of budgeting, cash flow management, and financial forecasting. By creating a detailed budget, you can track your expenses and ensure that your business stays on track financially. Additionally, learning how to manage cash flow effectively will help you maintain a healthy financial position, ensuring that you have enough capital to cover expenses and invest in growth opportunities.

In the age of social media, becoming a social media entrepreneur has become an attractive option for many young people. Building a personal brand and leveraging social media platforms can provide incredible opportunities for success. However, it is essential to approach this niche with a strategic mindset. Understanding the algorithms and analytics of various platforms, creating engaging content, and cultivating a loyal following are critical to building a successful social media presence.

For those aspiring to become sustainable entrepreneurs, combining passion for the environment with business acumen is key. Sustainable entrepreneurship involves creating ventures that prioritize environmental and social responsibility. To succeed in this niche, you must develop a deep understanding of sustainability practices, such as reducing waste, implementing renewable energy sources, and promoting ethical supply chains. Furthermore, building partnerships with like-minded organizations and staying informed about the latest sustainable trends will help you create a meaningful impact.

No matter which entrepreneurial path you choose, effective operations management is vital to ensure your business runs smoothly. This includes developing efficient processes, managing resources, and optimizing productivity. Implementing technology solutions, such as project management tools and customer relationship management systems, can streamline your operations and enhance efficiency.

In conclusion, managing finances and operations is an integral part of becoming a successful entrepreneur, regardless of the niche you choose. By mastering financial management, understanding the dynamics of social media entrepreneurship, and embracing sustainable practices, you will be well-equipped to break the mold and embark on a fulfilling entrepreneurial journey. Remember, entrepreneurship is not only about pursuing your passion but also about making a positive impact on the world around you.

Overcoming Obstacles and Staying Motivated

In the journey of entrepreneurship, it's inevitable to face obstacles and challenges that can test your determination and motivation. However, it's crucial to remember that these obstacles are not roadblocks but rather opportunities for growth and learning. In this subchapter, we will explore effective strategies for overcoming obstacles and staying motivated throughout your entrepreneurial endeavors.

One of the first steps to overcoming obstacles is to develop a resilient mindset. Understand that setbacks are a natural part of the entrepreneurial journey. Embrace them as valuable lessons and opportunities for personal and professional growth. Remember, the most successful entrepreneurs have faced numerous failures before achieving their goals.

Maintaining a clear vision and setting realistic goals is another essential aspect of staying motivated. Define your long-term vision and break it down into smaller, achievable goals. This will help you stay focused and motivated, as each milestone achieved will bring you closer to your ultimate vision.

Surrounding yourself with a supportive network is crucial when facing obstacles. Seek out mentors, peers, or like-minded individuals who can provide guidance and encouragement. They can offer valuable advice, share their experiences, and inspire you during challenging times.

Another effective strategy for overcoming obstacles is to develop problem-solving skills. Rather than dwelling on the problem, shift your mindset to finding solutions. Break down the obstacle into smaller, manageable tasks and brainstorm creative solutions. Remember, every problem has a solution; it's just a matter of finding it.

When it comes to becoming an entrepreneur in specific niches, such as social media or sustainability, there are additional challenges and opportunities to consider. For young people aspiring to become social media entrepreneurs, it's crucial to stay up-to-date with the latest trends and technologies. Embrace experimentation and continuously refine your strategies to leverage the power of social media platforms effectively.

For those interested in sustainable entrepreneurship, it's essential to align your business goals with environmental and social responsibilities. Seek innovative ways to create a positive impact while building a profitable business. Embrace sustainable practices, such as reducing waste and incorporating eco-friendly materials into your products or services.

In conclusion, overcoming obstacles and staying motivated are key factors in the journey of entrepreneurship. Develop a resilient mindset, set realistic goals, and surround yourself with a supportive network. Embrace challenges as opportunities for growth and continuously refine your problem-solving skills. For aspiring social media or sustainable entrepreneurs, stay up-to-date with trends and align your business goals with your niche's values. Remember, perseverance and motivation are the driving forces behind every successful entrepreneur.

Chapter 3: How to Become a Social Media Entrepreneur

Understanding the Power of Social Media

In today's digital age, social media has transformed the way we communicate, interact, and do business. It has become an integral part of our lives, influencing our decisions, shaping our opinions, and connecting us with people from all corners of the world. In this subchapter, we will delve into the power of social media and explore how it can be harnessed to become a successful entrepreneur, specifically focusing on becoming a social media entrepreneur and a sustainable entrepreneur.

Social media has revolutionized entrepreneurship by creating vast opportunities for young individuals to start and grow their businesses. Platforms like Facebook, Instagram, Twitter, and LinkedIn provide a global stage for entrepreneurs to showcase their products or services, build a strong brand presence, and reach a wide audience. The power of social media lies in its ability to connect businesses with potential customers, create brand awareness, and drive sales. By understanding and utilizing the various social media tools and strategies, young entrepreneurs can leverage this power to their advantage.

Becoming a social media entrepreneur involves mastering the art of creating engaging content, building a loyal following, and effectively utilizing social media platforms to monetize your business. This subchapter will guide you through the process of identifying your target audience, crafting compelling content, and implementing social media marketing strategies to grow your business. It will also highlight the importance of building authentic connections, engaging with your audience, and leveraging influencers to expand your reach.

Moreover, we will explore the concept of sustainable entrepreneurship, which focuses on building businesses that not only generate profits but also have a positive impact on society and the environment. Social media can play a vital role in promoting sustainable businesses, as it allows entrepreneurs to raise awareness about their sustainable practices, engage with like-minded individuals, and collaborate for a greater cause. We will discuss the principles of sustainable entrepreneurship, showcase successful sustainable businesses, and provide insights on how social media can be used to amplify their impact.

In conclusion, understanding the power of social media is crucial for young entrepreneurs aspiring to make their mark in today's digital world. By embracing social media as a tool for growth, young individuals can unlock their entrepreneurial potential, become successful social media entrepreneurs, and contribute to the sustainable development of our society and planet. So, dive into this subchapter and embark on your journey to entrepreneurial success through the power of social media.

Choosing the Right Social Media Platform

In this digital age, social media has become an integral part of our daily lives. It has also emerged as a powerful tool for entrepreneurs to connect with their target audience, build brand awareness, and drive business growth. However, with a plethora of social media platforms available, it can be overwhelming to determine which one is the right fit for your entrepreneurial journey. This subchapter will guide young aspiring entrepreneurs on how to choose the right social media platform to maximize their success.

When considering the right social media platform, it is essential to evaluate your target audience. Different platforms attract different demographics and user behaviors. For instance, Instagram is popular among younger audiences who appreciate visual content, while LinkedIn caters to professionals and businesses seeking networking opportunities. By understanding your target audience's preferences and demographics, you can select a platform that aligns with their interests and effectively engage with them.

Furthermore, it is crucial to consider your business goals and objectives. If you aim to showcase your creativity and visually appealing products, platforms like Instagram, Pinterest, or TikTok might be ideal. On the other hand, if you want to establish professional connections and share industry insights, LinkedIn and Twitter could be more suitable. Aligning your business goals with the platform's features and functionalities will ensure that you make the most of your social media presence.

Another factor to consider is the level of competition and saturation on each platform. Some platforms might be oversaturated with content, making it difficult for your business to stand out. Researching and analyzing the competition on different platforms will help you identify opportunities and niches that are less crowded, allowing you to gain a competitive edge.

Moreover, it is crucial to evaluate the resources and capabilities required to effectively manage and maintain your chosen platform. Each platform requires a different content strategy, format, and frequency. Consider your available time, budget, and skills to ensure that you can consistently produce high-quality content and engage with your audience.

Lastly, staying up-to-date with the latest trends and emerging platforms is essential. The social media landscape is constantly evolving, and new platforms are frequently introduced. Keeping an eye on emerging platforms and trends will help you adapt your strategies and stay ahead of the curve.

Choosing the right social media platform is a critical decision for young entrepreneurs. By considering factors such as target audience, business goals, competition, resources, and trends, you can make an informed choice that aligns with your entrepreneurial aspirations. Remember, the right platform can be a powerful tool to build your brand, connect with your audience, and propel your entrepreneurial journey forward.

Building a Strong Online Presence

In today's digital age, having a strong online presence is essential for anyone looking to become an entrepreneur. Whether you aspire to be a traditional entrepreneur, a social media entrepreneur, or a sustainable entrepreneur, establishing a robust online presence can significantly boost your chances of success. This subchapter will guide young people on how to build and maintain a strong online presence, regardless of their entrepreneurial niche.

To begin, it's crucial to understand the power of the internet and social media. Platforms like Facebook, Instagram, Twitter, and LinkedIn offer incredible opportunities to connect with potential customers, investors, and collaborators. By leveraging these platforms effectively, you can expand your reach, showcase your products or ideas, and build a strong network within your industry.

Start by creating professional profiles across various social media platforms. This includes using high-quality profile pictures, writing compelling bios, and sharing relevant and engaging content. Consistency is key; regularly update your profiles with new posts, articles, or videos to keep your audience engaged. Additionally, be responsive to messages and comments, as this shows your dedication to building relationships and providing excellent customer service.

To become a social media entrepreneur, it is vital to understand the algorithms and trends that shape these platforms. Stay up-to-date with the latest social media trends and adapt your content accordingly. Utilize hashtags, collaborations, and influencer marketing strategies to increase your visibility and attract a wider audience.

As a sustainable entrepreneur, it's crucial to communicate your mission and values effectively. Share content that showcases your commitment to sustainability and environmental responsibility. Engage with like-minded individuals, organizations, and communities to build a network that supports your cause. By establishing yourself as a reliable and reputable eco-conscious entrepreneur, you can attract customers who align with your values.

Lastly, regardless of your entrepreneurial niche, consider creating a professional website. A website serves as a central hub for your online presence, allowing you to showcase your products, services, or initiatives in a cohesive and organized manner. Optimize your website for search engines by incorporating relevant keywords and ensuring it is mobile-friendly.

Building a strong online presence is an ongoing process. Regularly evaluate your strategies, analyze your metrics, and adapt your approach accordingly. Embrace the power of social media, connect with industry leaders, and engage with your audience consistently. By doing so, you'll establish yourself as a credible and influential entrepreneur in your chosen field.

Creating Engaging Content

In today's digital age, creating engaging content is key to capturing the attention of your target audience and building a successful business. Whether you aspire to become an entrepreneur, a social media entrepreneur, or a sustainable entrepreneur, mastering the art of creating engaging content is a vital skill that can set you apart from the competition.

To begin with, it is important to understand what engaging content means. Engaging content is any form of media, such as blog posts, videos, or social media posts, that captures the interest and attention of your audience. It is content that leaves a lasting impression, sparks conversation, and encourages people to take action.

One of the first steps in creating engaging content is to know your audience. Research and understand the interests, needs, and preferences of your target market. This will help you tailor your content specifically to their wants and desires, making it more likely to resonate with them.

Next, focus on storytelling. Humans are naturally drawn to stories, so incorporating storytelling techniques into your content can make it more compelling and memorable. Share personal anecdotes, case studies, or success stories that relate to your brand or the problem your product or service solves. This will help your audience connect with your content on a deeper level.

Another important aspect of creating engaging content is to provide value. Your content should be informative, entertaining, or inspiring. It should offer something of worth to your audience, whether it's practical advice, insightful tips, or simply a good laugh. By consistently providing value, you can build trust and loyalty with your audience.

Additionally, visuals play a crucial role in capturing attention and creating engagement. Incorporate eye-catching images, graphics, or videos into your content to make it more visually appealing. Utilize platforms like Instagram, YouTube, or TikTok to showcase your content in a visually captivating way.

Lastly, remember to encourage interaction with your audience. Ask questions, invite comments, or create polls to prompt engagement. Respond to comments and messages promptly, showing that you value and appreciate their input. By fostering a sense of community and dialogue, you can keep your audience engaged and interested in your content.

In conclusion, creating engaging content is an essential skill for any aspiring entrepreneur. Whether you're looking to start a traditional business, become a social media influencer, or build a sustainable brand, captivating your audience through compelling content is crucial. By understanding your audience, telling engaging stories, providing value, utilizing visuals, and encouraging interaction, you can create content that captures attention, sparks conversation, and drives success in your entrepreneurial journey.

Growing Your Social Media Following

In today's digital age, social media has become an essential tool for entrepreneurs to promote their businesses and connect with their target audience. If you're a young person aspiring to become an entrepreneur, understanding how to grow your social media following can be a game-changer. In this subchapter, we will explore effective strategies that can help you build a strong and engaged online community.

1. Define Your Target Audience: Before diving into social media, identify your target audience. Who are they? What are their interests? Understanding your audience will allow you to tailor your content to their preferences and engage with them effectively.

2. Choose the Right Social Media Platforms: Not all social media platforms are created equal. Each platform has its own unique features and user demographics. Research which platforms align with your target audience and focus your efforts on those platforms. For example, if your business is visually-oriented, Instagram may be the best choice.

3. Create Quality Content: Content is king in the social media realm. Be consistent in delivering high-quality, valuable content that resonates with your audience. Whether it's informative blog posts, captivating visuals, or entertaining videos, your content should reflect your brand's personality and provide value to your followers.

4. Engage with Your Audience: Social media is all about building connections. Respond to comments, engage in conversations, and show genuine interest in your followers. By fostering a sense of community, you'll not only increase your following but also establish loyal customers who can become brand ambassadors.

5. Collaborate with Influencers: Influencer marketing is a powerful technique to expand your reach. Identify influencers within your niche who have a substantial following and collaborate with them. Their endorsement can introduce your brand to a wider audience and boost your credibility.

6. Utilize Hashtags: Hashtags are an effective way to increase your visibility on social media platforms. Research popular and relevant hashtags in your industry and incorporate them into your posts. This will help your content reach a broader audience and attract potential followers.

7. Analyze and Adapt: Monitor your social media performance regularly. Use analytics tools to analyze your engagement, reach, and follower growth. Identify what works and what doesn't, and adapt your strategy accordingly. A data-driven approach will help you optimize your social media efforts.

Remember, building a social media following takes time and effort. Be patient and consistent, and don't be afraid to experiment and learn from your experiences. By growing your social media following, you'll not only increase your brand's visibility but also create opportunities for business growth and success as a young entrepreneur.

Whether you're aiming to become a social media entrepreneur or a sustainable entrepreneur, mastering the art of growing your social media following is crucial in today's competitive business landscape. Embrace the power of social media and watch your entrepreneurial dreams take flight!

Collaborating with Influencers and Brands

In today's digital age, the world of entrepreneurship has expanded beyond traditional business models. Young people are now leveraging the power of social media to create their own paths as entrepreneurs. This subchapter aims to guide aspiring young entrepreneurs on how to collaborate with influencers and brands to achieve success in their ventures.

One of the most effective ways to gain visibility and reach a wider audience is by partnering with influencers. These individuals have established themselves as experts in their respective niches and have a dedicated following. Collaborating with influencers can provide young entrepreneurs with a valuable platform to showcase their products or services.

The first step in collaborating with influencers is to identify those who align with your brand and target audience. Conduct thorough research to ensure that their values, content, and audience match your business goals. Once you have a list of potential influencers, reach out to them with a personalized pitch explaining how collaborating with you can benefit both parties. Offer them a unique value proposition, such as exclusive discounts for their followers or the opportunity to co-create content.

When collaborating with influencers, it's crucial to establish clear expectations and goals from the outset. Clearly outline what you hope to achieve through the collaboration, whether it's increased brand awareness, product sales, or social media engagement. Establishing a mutually beneficial partnership will ensure a successful collaboration and build long-term relationships.

In addition to influencers, collaborating with established brands can also be advantageous for young entrepreneurs. Partnering with well-known brands can lend credibility to your venture and provide access to their existing customer base. However, it's essential to choose brands that align with your values and target audience to ensure a successful collaboration.

When approaching brands, highlight how your business can complement their offerings and add value to their customers. Emphasize your unique selling points and the potential benefits of a partnership. Remember that brands receive numerous collaboration requests, so make sure your pitch stands out by showcasing your creativity and passion.

Collaborating with influencers and brands is not only an excellent way to gain exposure but also an opportunity to learn and grow as an entrepreneur. By leveraging their expertise and networks, young entrepreneurs can accelerate their journey to success in the digital realm. However, it's crucial to approach collaborations with a clear plan, open communication, and mutual respect for a fruitful and sustainable partnership.

Monetizing Your Social Media Presence

In today's digital age, social media has become an integral part of our lives. It is not just a platform for connecting with friends and sharing our experiences; it has also emerged as a powerful tool for entrepreneurs to build their businesses. In this subchapter, we will explore how you can monetize your social media presence and turn it into a successful entrepreneurial venture.

Social media has opened up a world of opportunities for young people aspiring to become entrepreneurs. It has leveled the playing field, allowing anyone with a passion and dedication to build a business from scratch. Whether you want to become a social media influencer, start an online store, or provide services, social media offers an unrivaled platform to showcase your skills and connect with potential customers.

To become a social media entrepreneur, you need to start by identifying your niche and target audience. What are you passionate about? What unique skills or talents do you possess? Once you have a clear understanding of your strengths, you can develop a content strategy that resonates with your audience. Consistently creating high-quality and engaging content will help you build a loyal following, which is crucial for monetization.

One of the primary ways to monetize your social media presence is through brand collaborations and sponsorships. As your following grows, brands will start to notice your influence and reach out to collaborate with you. These partnerships can include sponsored posts, product placements, or even brand ambassadorships. However, it's essential to maintain authenticity and only collaborate with brands that align with your values and interests.

Another avenue for monetization is through selling products or services. If you have a unique product or skill, you can leverage your social media presence to promote and sell it. Many successful entrepreneurs have launched online stores, coaching programs, or digital products by utilizing the reach and influence of their social media platforms.

Lastly, to become a sustainable entrepreneur, it's crucial to diversify your income streams. Relying solely on one source of income can be risky. Consider exploring additional revenue streams, such as affiliate marketing, sponsored content, or creating exclusive paid content for your most dedicated followers.

In conclusion, monetizing your social media presence can be a game-changer for young entrepreneurs. By identifying your niche, creating engaging content, and building a loyal following, you can attract brand collaborations, sell products or services, and establish a sustainable business. However, remember that success on social media requires time, effort, and patience. Stay true to your vision, provide value to your audience, and embrace the ever-changing landscape of social media entrepreneurship.

Navigating Challenges and Staying Relevant

Subchapter: Navigating Challenges and Staying Relevant

Introduction:
Embarking on the journey of entrepreneurship can be both thrilling and daunting. As aspiring young entrepreneurs, you are undoubtedly filled with passion, ideas, and determination. However, you must also be prepared for the challenges that lie ahead. In this subchapter, we will delve into the strategies and mindset necessary to navigate these obstacles while staying relevant in your chosen entrepreneurial niche. Whether you aim to become a general entrepreneur, a social media entrepreneur, or a sustainable entrepreneur, the principles discussed here will be applicable and valuable to your journey.

1. Embrace the Uncertainty:
Entrepreneurship is an ever-evolving landscape, and being comfortable with uncertainty is crucial. Expect and embrace the unexpected, as it is often the catalyst for innovation and growth. By maintaining a flexible mindset, you can adapt to changing circumstances and seize new opportunities that arise.

2. Continuous Learning:

To stay relevant in today's fast-paced world, committing to lifelong learning is vital. Engage in constant self-improvement by reading books, attending seminars, and seeking mentorship from industry experts. By staying informed about emerging trends, technologies, and consumer preferences, you can position yourself as a knowledgeable and adaptable entrepreneur.

3. Networking and Collaboration:

Building a strong network of like-minded individuals and professionals within your niche is key to staying relevant. Attend industry events, join entrepreneurial communities, and actively seek out collaborations. By surrounding yourself with talented individuals, you can leverage their expertise and create innovative solutions together.

4. Embrace Technology:

In this digital age, technology plays a crucial role in entrepreneurship. For social media entrepreneurs, understanding various platforms, algorithms, and digital marketing strategies is essential. Sustainable entrepreneurs must explore technological advancements that can support their eco-friendly initiatives. Embrace technology as a tool to streamline your processes, reach a larger audience, and stay ahead of the curve.

5. Adaptability and Resilience:

Entrepreneurship is a journey filled with ups and downs. Being adaptable and resilient in the face of challenges is crucial. Learn from failures, iterate your ideas, and remain persistent in your pursuit of success. Embrace a growth mindset that allows you to learn from setbacks and use them as stepping stones toward future accomplishments.

Conclusion:

Navigating challenges and staying relevant in the entrepreneurial world requires a combination of adaptability, continuous learning, networking, and embracing technology. Whether you aspire to become a general entrepreneur, a social media entrepreneur, or a sustainable entrepreneur, the principles discussed in this subchapter will empower you to overcome obstacles and thrive in your chosen niche. Remember, success in entrepreneurship is not solely measured by financial gains but also by the positive impact you create in the world. By embodying these principles, you can break the mold and become a successful young entrepreneur.

Chapter 4: How to Become a Sustainable Entrepreneur

Understanding the Importance of Sustainability

In today's ever-changing world, it is crucial for young people to understand the importance of sustainability. Whether you aspire to become an entrepreneur, a social media influencer, or a sustainable entrepreneur, incorporating sustainable practices and values into your endeavors will not only benefit the planet but also contribute to your long-term success.

As an aspiring entrepreneur, you may wonder why sustainability matters. Well, sustainability is all about finding ways to meet the needs of the present generation without compromising the ability of future generations to meet their own needs. By considering the environmental, social, and economic impacts of your business, you can create a venture that not only generates profit but also has a positive impact on society and the environment.

If your goal is to become a social media entrepreneur, sustainability should be a key aspect of your content and brand strategy. By promoting sustainable products, sharing eco-friendly tips, or advocating for social causes, you can engage your audience and build a loyal community that shares your values. Remember, young people today are increasingly conscious of the impact their choices have on the world, and they are more likely to support brands that align with their values.

For those interested in becoming sustainable entrepreneurs, you have a unique opportunity to create businesses that are both profitable and environmentally friendly. By developing sustainable products or services, implementing green practices, and prioritizing ethical sourcing and manufacturing, you can differentiate your business and attract conscious consumers who actively seek out sustainable options.

Furthermore, embracing sustainability can also lead to cost savings and operational efficiencies. By adopting energy-efficient technologies, reducing waste, and optimizing resource consumption, you can lower your business's expenses while minimizing its ecological footprint.

In conclusion, understanding the importance of sustainability is essential for young people aspiring to become entrepreneurs, social media influencers, or sustainable entrepreneurs. By incorporating sustainable practices and values into your ventures, you can not only contribute to a better future but also attract like-minded individuals, build a loyal customer base, and achieve long-term success. So, embrace sustainability and let it guide your entrepreneurial journey towards a brighter and more sustainable future for all.

Identifying Sustainable Business Opportunities

In today's rapidly changing world, the desire to become an entrepreneur is more prevalent than ever among young people. But how do you identify sustainable business opportunities? This subchapter will guide you through the process of recognizing and capitalizing on entrepreneurial ventures that align with your passions and values.

Entrepreneurship is not just about making money; it's about creating a positive impact on society and the environment. As a young person, you have the unique advantage of being connected to various niche markets and having a deep understanding of the needs and preferences of your generation. This subchapter will explore three specific niches: how to become an entrepreneur, how to become a social media entrepreneur, and how to become a sustainable entrepreneur.

To become an entrepreneur, start by identifying your passions and areas of expertise. What problems do you see in the world that you could solve? Conduct market research to understand trends and potential target audiences. Explore your network and seek mentorship from experienced entrepreneurs who can guide you through the process. Remember, failure is a part of the journey, so embrace it and learn from your experiences.

If your interests lie in the realm of social media, becoming a social media entrepreneur can be a viable path. With the rise of digital platforms, there are endless opportunities to create content, build a brand, and monetize your online presence. This subchapter will provide insights into how to identify your niche, engage with your audience, and collaborate with brands to generate revenue.

For those passionate about sustainability and making a positive impact on the environment, becoming a sustainable entrepreneur is the way to go. This subchapter will explore the growing demand for eco-friendly products and services, as well as the importance of incorporating sustainable practices into your business model. Learn about green certifications, renewable energy sources, and ethical sourcing to ensure your business aligns with your values.

In summary, this subchapter is designed to help young people like you identify sustainable business opportunities in various niches. Whether you aspire to become a general entrepreneur, a social media entrepreneur, or a sustainable entrepreneur, the principles and strategies discussed here will guide you towards success. Remember, entrepreneurship is not just about making money; it's about creating a better world for future generations. Embrace your passions, seek knowledge, and take action to become the entrepreneur you aspire to be.

Incorporating Green Practices into Your Business

As a young person with aspirations of becoming an entrepreneur, you possess the power to make a significant impact on the world. One way to achieve this is by incorporating green practices into your business model. Not only will this help you stand out in a competitive market, but it will also contribute to building a sustainable future for generations to come.

Becoming an entrepreneur means taking risks, thinking outside the box, and exploring innovative ideas. So why not apply this mindset to promote environmental sustainability? Here are some key steps to help you incorporate green practices into your business:

1. Embrace sustainable products and services: Opt for eco-friendly alternatives in every aspect of your business. From sourcing materials to manufacturing and packaging, prioritize suppliers who prioritize sustainability. This way, you can offer products and services that align with your values and attract environmentally conscious customers.

2. Reduce, reuse, recycle: Implement effective waste management strategies within your organization. Encourage employees to reduce paper usage, recycle materials, and reuse resources whenever possible. By adopting a circular economy approach, you can minimize your carbon footprint and contribute to a greener planet.

3. Harness the power of technology: Leverage technology to streamline your operations and reduce energy consumption. Implement digital tools and software to optimize processes, minimize paper usage, and reduce travel requirements. Utilize cloud-based solutions to store data, reducing the need for physical storage spaces and cutting down on energy consumption.

4. Collaborate with like-minded organizations: Seek partnerships with other businesses that share your commitment to sustainability. Collaborating with environmental organizations, NGOs, or social enterprises can amplify your impact and help you reach a wider audience. Together, you can develop innovative solutions to pressing environmental challenges.

5. Educate and engage your customers: Inform your customers about the environmental benefits of choosing your products or services. Use your social media platforms to raise awareness about sustainability and share tips on how they can make a difference in their daily lives. Engage with your audience through interactive campaigns and encourage them to join your mission.

By incorporating green practices into your business, you can not only create a successful venture but also align your passion for entrepreneurship with your desire to make a positive impact on the world. Remember, being a sustainable entrepreneur is about more than just profits; it's about leaving a lasting legacy that inspires others to follow in your footsteps. So go ahead, break the mold, and build a business that not only thrives but also contributes to a greener, more sustainable future.

Building a Sustainable Supply Chain

In today's fast-paced business world, building a sustainable supply chain is crucial for entrepreneurs who want to make a positive impact on the world. A sustainable supply chain ensures that products and services are sourced, produced, and distributed in an environmentally and socially responsible manner. This subchapter aims to provide young people interested in entrepreneurship with insights and strategies to create a sustainable supply chain.

To become an entrepreneur, you must first understand the concept of sustainability. Sustainability encompasses not only environmental factors but also social and economic aspects. It means considering the long-term impacts of your business decisions on the planet, people, and profits. By integrating sustainable practices into your supply chain, you can minimize your carbon footprint, support local communities, and contribute to a healthier planet.

If you aspire to become a social media entrepreneur, you have the power to leverage your online presence to promote sustainability. Use your platform to educate and inspire others about the importance of sustainable practices. Share stories of businesses that are making a difference and showcase how their sustainable supply chains contribute to their success. By engaging your audience on social media, you can create a community of like-minded individuals who are passionate about sustainability.

Becoming a sustainable entrepreneur involves taking a holistic approach to your supply chain. Start by evaluating your current practices and identifying areas for improvement. Consider sourcing materials locally to reduce transportation emissions and support local economies. Opt for eco-friendly packaging and shipping methods to minimize waste. Collaborate with suppliers who adhere to ethical labor practices and prioritize fair trade. These small changes can have a significant impact on your sustainability efforts.

It is also essential to forge partnerships with like-minded organizations and suppliers who share your commitment to sustainability. By working together, you can amplify your impact and create a network of businesses that support each other's sustainable goals. Collaborate on initiatives and projects that benefit the environment and the community, such as tree planting campaigns or recycling programs.

Remember, building a sustainable supply chain is an ongoing process. Continuously evaluate and improve your practices to stay at the forefront of sustainability. By aligning your business with sustainable principles, you can create a positive impact and inspire others to do the same. As a young entrepreneur, you have the opportunity to shape the future and build a sustainable world for generations to come.

Educating and Engaging Your Customers

In the fast-paced world of entrepreneurship, it is essential to understand the importance of educating and engaging your customers. As a young person venturing into the world of entrepreneurship, you must realize that your success lies in the hands of your customers. By building a strong connection with them, you can not only gain their loyalty but also create a community around your brand. This subchapter will delve into the strategies you can employ to educate and engage your customers, regardless of whether you aspire to become a general entrepreneur, a social media entrepreneur, or a sustainable entrepreneur.

First and foremost, it is vital to understand your target audience. Conduct thorough market research to identify their needs, preferences, and pain points. By understanding your customers inside out, you can tailor your products or services to meet their specific requirements. This approach not only increases customer satisfaction but also helps you stand out from the competition.

Once you have a solid understanding of your audience, it's time to educate them about your brand and offerings. This can be done through various channels such as social media, blogs, podcasts, or even hosting webinars. Create valuable content that educates and provides insights to your customers, positioning yourself as an expert in your niche. By sharing your knowledge and expertise, you not only establish credibility but also build trust with your customers.

Engagement is the key to building a loyal customer base. Encourage your customers to provide feedback, reviews, and testimonials. Implement strategies that foster two-way communication, such as responding promptly to inquiries or conducting surveys to gather customer opinions. By actively engaging with your customers, you create a sense of community and make them feel valued.

For those aspiring to become social media entrepreneurs, platforms like Instagram, YouTube, and TikTok are powerful tools for customer education and engagement. Utilize these platforms to showcase your products or services, share behind-the-scenes content, and interact directly with your audience. Harness the power of social media influencers and collaborations to expand your reach and connect with potential customers.

For those interested in becoming sustainable entrepreneurs, educate your customers about the importance of sustainability and eco-friendly practices. Share the impact your business has on the environment and highlight the steps you are taking to minimize it. Engage your customers by involving them in sustainable initiatives, such as recycling programs or planting trees for each purchase made. By aligning your brand with sustainability, you not only attract like-minded customers but also contribute to a better future.

In conclusion, educating and engaging your customers is crucial for success in entrepreneurship. Regardless of your niche, understanding your target audience, providing valuable content, and fostering strong relationships are the key ingredients to building a loyal customer base. Embrace the power of technology and social media to amplify your efforts and create a community around your brand. Remember, your customers are the driving force behind your success, so invest time and effort in connecting with them on a deeper level.

Measuring and Reporting Your Environmental Impact

As an aspiring young entrepreneur, it is crucial to understand the concept of measuring and reporting your environmental impact. In today's world, where sustainability is gaining increasing importance, entrepreneurs have a responsibility to ensure their businesses operate in an environmentally conscious manner. This subchapter will equip you with the necessary knowledge to assess and communicate your environmental impact effectively.

Measuring your environmental impact involves quantifying the positive or negative effects your business has on the environment. This can be done through various means, such as tracking energy consumption, waste generation, water usage, and carbon emissions. By collecting this data, you can gain insights into your business's environmental performance and identify areas for improvement.

To become a successful entrepreneur, it is essential to understand how your specific niche intersects with environmental sustainability. Whether you aspire to become a general entrepreneur, a social media entrepreneur, or a sustainable entrepreneur, integrating sustainability into your business model can set you apart from the competition.

For those interested in becoming a social media entrepreneur, you can leverage your platform to raise awareness about environmental issues and promote sustainable practices. By measuring and reporting your environmental impact, you can demonstrate your commitment to sustainability and inspire your audience to make eco-conscious choices.

Becoming a sustainable entrepreneur requires a deep understanding of the environmental impact of your business operations. By employing sustainable practices, such as sourcing eco-friendly materials, implementing energy-efficient technologies, and minimizing waste, you can effectively reduce your ecological footprint. Measuring and reporting on these efforts will not only help you monitor progress but also attract like-minded customers who prioritize sustainability.

Reporting your environmental impact is key to transparency and accountability. By sharing your sustainability initiatives, accomplishments, and goals, you can build trust with your stakeholders, including customers, investors, and the wider community. Additionally, reporting can lead to partnerships and collaborations with organizations that share your environmental values.

In conclusion, measuring and reporting your environmental impact is an integral part of being a successful and responsible entrepreneur. By understanding the significance of sustainability in your chosen niche, you can make informed decisions to minimize your ecological footprint. Embracing sustainability not only benefits the environment but also enhances your brand reputation and attracts environmentally conscious customers. Remember, as a young entrepreneur, you have the power to create positive change and shape a more sustainable future.

Collaborating with Like-Minded Organizations

In the fast-paced world of entrepreneurship, collaboration is key. As a young entrepreneur, building connections and working with like-minded organizations can significantly enhance your chances of success. By joining forces with others who share your passion and vision, you can tap into a wealth of resources, knowledge, and expertise that will propel your journey to becoming a successful entrepreneur.

When it comes to collaborating with like-minded organizations, there are several avenues you can explore. Here are some valuable insights for young people interested in different niches of entrepreneurship, including how to become an entrepreneur, a social media entrepreneur, or a sustainable entrepreneur.

1. How to become an entrepreneur:
Collaborating with other entrepreneurs who have already established successful businesses can be immensely beneficial. Seek out mentorship programs, startup incubators, or entrepreneurship communities where you can connect with experienced individuals who are willing to share their knowledge and guide you through the challenges of starting your own venture. By leveraging their expertise, you can avoid common pitfalls and gain valuable insights that can fast-track your entrepreneurial journey.

2. How to become a social media entrepreneur:
In the digital age, social media entrepreneurship has become a popular niche. To thrive in this field, it is crucial to collaborate with like-minded organizations that align with your brand values and target audience. Partnering with influencers, content creators, or other businesses in your industry can help you expand your reach, enhance your brand's visibility, and tap into new markets. Additionally, collaborating with social media management platforms or agencies can streamline your operations, allowing you to focus on creating compelling content and engaging with your audience.

3. How to become a sustainable entrepreneur:
Sustainability is a growing concern in today's world, and many young entrepreneurs are keen to make a positive impact on the environment. Collaborating with like-minded organizations that prioritize sustainability can amplify your efforts and create a stronger collective impact. Seek partnerships with eco-friendly suppliers, green organizations, or sustainable-focused investors who can provide guidance, support, and resources to help you build a business that aligns with your values and contributes to a more sustainable future.

Remember, collaboration is not just about what you can gain; it is also about what you can contribute. Be open to sharing your expertise and resources with others, as this fosters a culture of reciprocity and strengthens the entrepreneurial ecosystem. By collaborating with like-minded organizations, you can create a network of support, expand your knowledge base, and increase your chances of long-term success as a young entrepreneur.

Adapting to Changing Sustainability Trends

In today's rapidly changing world, it is crucial for aspiring young entrepreneurs to stay ahead of the curve and adapt to the evolving sustainability trends. The concept of sustainability has become a global phenomenon, and businesses that embrace sustainable practices not only contribute to a better future but also thrive in the marketplace. As a young person aspiring to become an entrepreneur, it is essential to understand the significance of sustainability and how to incorporate it into your entrepreneurial journey.

To become an entrepreneur, you must first understand the fundamentals of entrepreneurship. It involves identifying a problem or a need in society and developing an innovative solution to address it. However, it is equally important to consider the impact of your business on the environment and society as a whole. Incorporating sustainability into your business model can help you create a positive impact while also attracting socially-conscious customers.

Becoming a social media entrepreneur is an exciting avenue to explore, especially in this digital age. Social media platforms have become powerful tools to reach and engage with a wide audience. As a social media entrepreneur, you have the opportunity to leverage these platforms to promote sustainability and influence positive change. By creating content that educates and inspires others to adopt sustainable practices, you can build a loyal following and establish yourself as a thought leader in this niche.

To become a sustainable entrepreneur, you need to develop a mindset that prioritizes environmental and social responsibility. It involves considering the entire lifecycle of your products or services and making conscious choices to minimize their negative impact. For instance, you can opt for renewable energy sources, reduce waste, and promote fair trade practices. By aligning your business goals with sustainable practices, you not only contribute to a greener planet but also attract environmentally-conscious customers who are willing to support your brand.

Adapting to changing sustainability trends requires continuous learning and staying updated with the latest innovations and practices. As a young entrepreneur, it is essential to network with like-minded individuals, attend conferences, and engage in online communities focused on sustainability. By staying connected to this evolving landscape, you can identify emerging trends and integrate them into your business strategy.

In conclusion, adapting to changing sustainability trends is an essential aspect of becoming a successful entrepreneur in today's world. Whether you choose to become a general entrepreneur, a social media entrepreneur, or a sustainable entrepreneur, incorporating sustainability into your business model will not only contribute to a better future but also help you stand out in the competitive marketplace. Embrace sustainability as a core value and use it as an opportunity to make a positive impact while pursuing your entrepreneurial dreams.

Chapter 5: Overcoming Age-related Challenges in Entrepreneurship

Dealing with Stereotypes and Prejudice

Stereotypes and prejudice are unfortunate realities that many young entrepreneurs face in their journey towards success. It is disheartening to be judged solely based on societal biases rather than one's capabilities and potential. However, it is crucial to remember that these obstacles can be overcome with resilience and determination.

Firstly, it is essential for young entrepreneurs to recognize that stereotypes exist and can affect their entrepreneurial endeavors. This awareness allows them to develop a strong sense of self and confidence in their abilities. By understanding that stereotypes are often based on assumptions rather than facts, young entrepreneurs can challenge these preconceived notions and prove them wrong through their actions and achievements.

One effective strategy for dealing with stereotypes and prejudice is to surround oneself with a supportive network of like-minded individuals. Seek out mentors, peers, and role models who have overcome similar challenges and can provide guidance and encouragement. Building a community of individuals who understand and appreciate your unique journey will provide the motivation and support needed to push through difficult times.

Another important aspect is education. Educating oneself and others about the power of diversity and inclusion is key to breaking down stereotypes and prejudice. By actively promoting diversity in your own entrepreneurial ventures, whether it be through hiring practices or collaborations, you can set an example for others to follow. Emphasizing that success comes from embracing different perspectives and backgrounds can help break the mold of traditional stereotypes.

Additionally, young entrepreneurs should not be afraid to speak up and stand against stereotyping and prejudice when they encounter it. By addressing these issues head-on, they can challenge the status quo and create a more inclusive and accepting environment for themselves and others. This can be done through public speaking engagements, social media campaigns, or even engaging in dialogues with industry leaders and policymakers.

In conclusion, dealing with stereotypes and prejudice is an unfortunate reality for many young entrepreneurs. However, by acknowledging and challenging these biases, building a supportive network, promoting diversity, and speaking up against injustice, young entrepreneurs can break free from societal constraints and pave their own path towards success. Remember, you have the power to shape your own narrative and redefine what it means to be an entrepreneur in today's world.

Building Credibility and Gaining Trust

In the world of entrepreneurship, credibility and trust are essential for success. Whether you want to become an entrepreneur, a social media entrepreneur, or a sustainable entrepreneur, building credibility and gaining trust should be at the forefront of your mind. In this subchapter, we will explore why credibility and trust are crucial, and provide practical tips on how to establish yourself as a reliable and trustworthy entrepreneur.

Credibility is the foundation upon which your business will thrive. It is the measure of your expertise, experience, and knowledge in your chosen field. As a young person entering the entrepreneurial world, you may face skepticism from potential clients or investors. Therefore, it is crucial to showcase your credibility from the start. One way to do this is by gaining relevant education or certifications in your field. Taking courses, attending workshops, or obtaining a degree can bolster your credibility and demonstrate your commitment to learning and growth.

Trust, on the other hand, is the glue that holds your relationships with customers, partners, and stakeholders together. Trust is built over time through consistent and ethical behavior. Honesty, transparency, and reliability are key components of trustworthiness. Be authentic and genuine in your interactions with others, and always deliver on your promises. Building a strong online presence and maintaining an active and engaged social media presence can also help establish trust with your audience.

To gain credibility and trust, it is essential to continuously demonstrate your expertise. Share your knowledge through content creation, such as blog posts, videos, or podcasts. Position yourself as a thought leader in your niche by providing valuable insights and solutions to common problems. Engage with your audience by responding to comments and questions, and actively seek feedback to show that you value their opinions.

Collaborating with established entrepreneurs or industry experts can also enhance your credibility. Seek mentorship from experienced individuals who can guide you and vouch for your skills and abilities. Collaborative projects and partnerships can also help you gain exposure and credibility within your industry.

Lastly, always deliver exceptional products or services. Consistently exceeding customer expectations will not only build trust but also generate positive word-of-mouth recommendations, which are invaluable for any entrepreneur.

Building credibility and gaining trust takes time and dedication. It is an ongoing process that requires consistent effort and a commitment to ethical practices. By focusing on these aspects, you will establish yourself as a reliable and trustworthy entrepreneur, paving the way for long-term success in your chosen niche.

Leveraging Your Youthful Advantage

As a young person, you have a unique advantage when it comes to entrepreneurship. Your energy, creativity, and willingness to take risks set you apart from other age groups. In this subchapter, we will explore how you can leverage your youthful advantage to become a successful entrepreneur, whether you're interested in starting a traditional business, becoming a social media entrepreneur, or focusing on sustainable entrepreneurship.

1. Embrace innovation and think outside the box: Young people are known for their fresh perspectives and ability to think outside the box. Use this to your advantage by constantly seeking innovative solutions to existing problems. Look for gaps in the market and find ways to fill them with your unique ideas. Don't be afraid to take risks and challenge conventional wisdom. Remember, some of the most successful businesses today were born out of young entrepreneurs' unconventional thinking.

2. Harness the power of technology and social media: In today's digital age, having a strong online presence is crucial for any entrepreneur. If you're interested in becoming a social media entrepreneur, embrace platforms like Instagram, YouTube, TikTok, and LinkedIn to showcase your skills and build a personal brand. Use social media to connect with your target audience, promote your products or services, and establish yourself as an industry expert. Leverage your familiarity with technology to your advantage and stay ahead of the curve.

3. Prioritize sustainability and social impact: Young people are increasingly passionate about social and environmental issues. Use your entrepreneurial skills to make a positive impact on the world. Consider becoming a sustainable entrepreneur by developing eco-friendly products or services. Incorporate ethical practices into your business model and prioritize social responsibility. Not only will this attract like-minded customers, but it will also give you a sense of purpose and fulfillment in your entrepreneurial journey.

4. Network and collaborate: As a young entrepreneur, building a strong network is crucial. Attend industry events, join entrepreneurship clubs or organizations, and connect with like-minded individuals. Seek out mentorship opportunities from experienced entrepreneurs who can guide you in your journey. Collaborate with other young entrepreneurs to share ideas, resources, and support. Remember, the power of networking can open doors to new opportunities and help you grow your business faster.

In conclusion, being a young entrepreneur opens up a world of possibilities. Embrace your youthful advantage by thinking innovatively, leveraging technology, prioritizing sustainability, and building strong relationships. By doing so, you can break the mold and pave your own path to success in whichever entrepreneurial niche you choose. Good luck on your journey!

Seeking Mentorship and Guidance

In the world of entrepreneurship, seeking mentorship and guidance is a crucial step towards achieving your goals. No matter which niche of entrepreneurship you are interested in – be it starting your own business, becoming a social media entrepreneur, or creating a sustainable venture – having a mentor can make all the difference. This subchapter aims to highlight the importance of seeking mentorship and guidance and provide valuable advice on how to find the right mentor for your journey.

Mentors play a vital role in shaping your entrepreneurial path. They offer insights and advice based on their own experiences, helping you navigate the challenges and uncertainties that lie ahead. A mentor can provide you with a fresh perspective, help you set realistic goals, and guide you towards making informed decisions. They can also connect you with valuable networks and resources that can accelerate your entrepreneurial journey.

To become an entrepreneur, it is essential to seek out mentors who have expertise in your chosen field. Look for individuals who have achieved success in the same industry or have a strong understanding of the challenges you may face. Attend networking events, join industry-specific groups, and utilize online platforms to connect with potential mentors. Reach out to them and express your interest in learning from their experiences. Remember, a mentorship relationship is a two-way street, so be prepared to offer your time and support in return.

For those interested in becoming a social media entrepreneur, finding a mentor who has successfully built an online presence can be invaluable. They can guide you on creating engaging content, growing your audience, and monetizing your social media platforms. Seek out mentors who have a deep understanding of the ever-evolving social media landscape and can help you navigate the intricacies of building a brand online.

If your goal is to become a sustainable entrepreneur, look for mentors who have expertise in environmentally friendly practices and sustainable business models. They can guide you on incorporating sustainability into your business plan, sourcing eco-friendly materials, and connecting with like-minded organizations. A mentor with a strong background in sustainability can help you align your values with your entrepreneurial endeavors, making a positive impact on both the environment and society.

In conclusion, seeking mentorship and guidance is a vital step for young entrepreneurs in all niches. Mentors provide valuable insights, support, and connections that can fast-track your path to success. Take the time to find mentors who align with your goals and values, and be open to learning from their experiences. Remember, the journey of entrepreneurship is not meant to be walked alone, and with the right mentor by your side, you can break the mold and create your own path to success.

Balancing Education and Entrepreneurship

In today's rapidly changing world, young people are increasingly drawn towards the allure of entrepreneurship. The desire to be your own boss, follow your passion, and make a difference in the world has never been more prominent. However, many young minds find themselves torn between pursuing their education and diving headfirst into the world of entrepreneurship. This subchapter aims to address the challenges and provide guidance on how to successfully balance education and entrepreneurship.

How to Become an Entrepreneur?

Becoming an entrepreneur is an exciting journey that requires a combination of passion, perseverance, and knowledge. While education plays a vital role in developing critical skills and knowledge, it is equally essential to gain practical experience in the entrepreneurial field. This subchapter explores strategies to effectively manage your time, set achievable goals, and leverage educational opportunities that align with your entrepreneurial aspirations.

How to Become a Social Media Entrepreneur?

Social media has revolutionized the way businesses connect with their target audience. Young people today have a unique advantage in understanding the intricacies of various social media platforms. This subchapter delves into the world of social media entrepreneurship, providing insights on building a personal brand, creating engaging content, and leveraging social media channels to grow your business. It also highlights the importance of continuous learning to stay updated with the ever-evolving social media landscape.

How to Become a Sustainable Entrepreneur?

With the increasing focus on environmental sustainability, many young individuals aspire to become entrepreneurs who make a positive impact on the planet. This subchapter explores the concept of sustainable entrepreneurship, emphasizing the need to balance economic growth with environmental and social responsibility. It provides guidance on identifying sustainable business opportunities, adopting eco-friendly practices, and building a brand that aligns with the values of sustainability.

Finding the Balance

Balancing education and entrepreneurship can be a daunting task, but it is not impossible. This subchapter offers practical tips and strategies to manage your time effectively, prioritize tasks, and maintain a healthy work-life balance. It emphasizes the importance of seeking mentorship, networking with like-minded individuals, and taking advantage of available resources to support your entrepreneurial journey.

In conclusion, the subchapter "Balancing Education and Entrepreneurship" provides young people with valuable insights and guidance on how to pursue their entrepreneurial dreams while continuing their education. It covers various niches, including general entrepreneurship, social media entrepreneurship, and sustainable entrepreneurship, catering to the diverse interests of aspiring young entrepreneurs. By striking the right balance and leveraging educational opportunities, young individuals can embark on a successful entrepreneurial journey without compromising their education.

Managing Time and Priorities

In the fast-paced world we live in, managing time and priorities is a crucial skill for any entrepreneur. As a young person eager to embark on the entrepreneurial journey, it is essential to understand how to effectively manage your time and prioritize your tasks. This subchapter will provide you with valuable insights and strategies to help you stay organized, focused, and productive.

1. Set Clear Goals: Begin by setting clear and specific goals for yourself. What do you want to achieve as an entrepreneur? Write down your goals and break them down into smaller, manageable tasks. This will help you stay motivated and focused on what needs to be done.

2. Create a Schedule: Develop a schedule that works for you. Allocate specific time slots for different activities, such as brainstorming, research, networking, and executing your business plans. Make sure to include breaks and downtime to maintain a healthy work-life balance.

3. Prioritize Tasks: Not all tasks hold the same level of importance. Learn to prioritize your tasks based on urgency and impact. Focus on high-priority tasks that align with your goals and will have a significant impact on your business.

4. Avoid Procrastination: Procrastination can be a major hurdle for young entrepreneurs. Combat it by breaking tasks into smaller, manageable steps and setting deadlines for each step. Hold yourself accountable and reward yourself upon completing tasks.

5. Delegate and Outsource: As an entrepreneur, you cannot do everything yourself. Identify tasks that can be delegated or outsourced to free up your time for more critical activities. Surround yourself with a reliable team and utilize freelancers or virtual assistants when needed.

6. Embrace Technology: Leverage technology to streamline your workflow and improve productivity. Use project management tools, time-tracking apps, and automation software to optimize your time management.

7. Learn to Say No: While it is essential to seize opportunities, learn to say no to tasks or projects that do not align with your goals or may distract you from your core objectives. Focus on activities that will contribute to your entrepreneurial journey.

Remember, time is a valuable resource, and effective time management is the key to your success as a young entrepreneur. By setting goals, creating a schedule, prioritizing tasks, avoiding procrastination, delegating, embracing technology, and learning to say no, you will be well on your way to becoming a successful entrepreneur.

Whether you aspire to be a general entrepreneur, a social media entrepreneur, or a sustainable entrepreneur, these time management and prioritization skills are applicable to all niches. Stay focused, stay organized, and stay driven on your entrepreneurial path.

Developing Strong Decision-making Skills

In the world of entrepreneurship, one of the most crucial skills you can possess is the ability to make strong and informed decisions. As a young person with dreams of becoming an entrepreneur, it is essential to develop this skill to navigate the challenges and uncertainties that come with starting your own business. Whether you aspire to become a traditional entrepreneur, a social media entrepreneur, or a sustainable entrepreneur, honing your decision-making skills will be the key to your success.

So, how can you develop strong decision-making skills? The first step is to gather as much information as possible. This means immersing yourself in your chosen field, reading books, attending workshops, and networking with industry professionals. The more knowledge you have, the better equipped you will be to make informed decisions.

Another important aspect of decision-making is the ability to analyze and evaluate different options. This involves assessing the pros and cons of each choice and considering the potential risks and rewards. It's crucial to think critically and objectively, weighing all the factors before making a final decision. Remember, every decision you make as an entrepreneur has the potential to impact your business, so take the time to analyze your choices thoroughly.

Furthermore, it is essential to trust your instincts. While gathering information and analyzing options are crucial, sometimes the best decisions come from your gut feeling. As a young entrepreneur, you possess a unique perspective and intuition that can guide you in the right direction. Trust yourself and have confidence in your abilities to make sound decisions.

Lastly, learn from your mistakes. Entrepreneurship is a journey filled with ups and downs, and you will undoubtedly encounter failures along the way. However, it is through these failures that you can grow and develop your decision-making skills. Reflect on your past decisions, identify where you went wrong, and use those experiences as lessons for the future. Embrace failure as an opportunity for growth and improvement.

In conclusion, developing strong decision-making skills is essential for any young person aspiring to become an entrepreneur. Whether you want to venture into traditional entrepreneurship, social media entrepreneurship, or sustainable entrepreneurship, the ability to make informed and effective decisions will set you apart from the competition. Gather knowledge, analyze options, trust your instincts, and learn from your mistakes. By doing so, you will become a confident and successful entrepreneur, ready to break the mold and create your own path in the business world.

Celebrating Successes and Learning from Failures

Subchapter: Celebrating Successes and Learning from Failures

Introduction:

In the journey of entrepreneurship, success and failure are two sides of the same coin. While success brings joy and a sense of accomplishment, failure can be disheartening and demotivating. However, both successes and failures are essential in shaping us as entrepreneurs. They are not just mere outcomes but valuable lessons that help us grow and refine our entrepreneurial skills. In this subchapter, we will delve into the importance of celebrating successes and learning from failures, regardless of the niche you choose to pursue – whether it's becoming an entrepreneur, a social media entrepreneur, or a sustainable entrepreneur.

1. Acknowledging Successes:

Successes, big or small, should be celebrated. They represent milestones and achievements on your entrepreneurial journey. Celebrating successes helps boost your confidence, provides motivation, and encourages you to keep pushing forward. Whether it's securing your first client, launching a successful marketing campaign, or hitting a revenue target, take the time to acknowledge and appreciate your accomplishments. Share your achievements with your peers, mentors, and loved ones, as their support can make your successes even more meaningful.

2. Embracing Failures:

Failure is an inevitable part of entrepreneurship, and it is crucial to view it as a learning opportunity rather than a setback. Failed ventures, unsuccessful marketing strategies, or rejected ideas should be embraced as stepping stones to success. Analyse your failures, identify the areas that went wrong, and learn from them. Failure teaches resilience, adaptability, and problem-solving skills – all of which are vital qualities for any entrepreneur. Remember, even the most successful entrepreneurs have faced failures along their journey.

3. Learning from Mistakes:

In the entrepreneurial world, mistakes are valuable lessons in disguise. Take the time to reflect on your failures and identify the lessons they offer. Did you underestimate the market demand? Did you fail to understand your target audience? Did you lack proper planning? By analyzing your mistakes, you can avoid making the same errors in the future. Learning from your mistakes helps you refine your strategies, make informed decisions, and ultimately increases your chances of success.

4. Cultivating a Growth Mindset:

To become a successful entrepreneur, it is essential to develop a growth mindset – the belief that one's abilities and intelligence can be developed through dedication and hard work. Celebrating successes and learning from failures contribute to this mindset by fostering resilience, determination, and a willingness to adapt. Embrace challenges, seek feedback, and continuously seek opportunities for personal and professional growth.

Conclusion:

Celebrating successes and learning from failures are integral parts of the entrepreneurial journey, regardless of the niche you choose to pursue. By acknowledging your achievements, embracing failures, and learning from mistakes, you can develop the mindset and skills necessary to succeed as an entrepreneur. Remember, success is not a destination but a continuous process of growth and learning.

Chapter 6: Case Studies of Young Successful Entrepreneurs

Entrepreneur A: From Idea to Success

In this subchapter of "Breaking the Mold: A Young Person's Guide to Entrepreneurship," we will explore the journey of Entrepreneur A, who started with just an idea and transformed it into a resounding success. Whether you aspire to become an entrepreneur, a social media entrepreneur, or a sustainable entrepreneur, Entrepreneur A's story will inspire and guide you on your own path to success.

Entrepreneurship is all about turning ideas into reality. Entrepreneur A began their journey with a simple idea, driven by passion and a desire to make a difference. They understood that the first step towards success was to take their idea seriously and develop a strong foundation.

To become an entrepreneur, you must start by identifying a problem or an opportunity. Entrepreneur A recognized a gap in the market and saw the potential to offer a unique solution. They conducted thorough market research, analyzed competitors, and built a solid business plan to turn their idea into a viable venture.

For those interested in becoming a social media entrepreneur, Entrepreneur A's story offers valuable insights. They understood the power of social media platforms and leveraged them to build a strong online presence. With a well-crafted social media strategy, they engaged with their target audience, built a community, and effectively marketed their products or services. They recognized the importance of staying up-to-date with the latest trends and adapting their strategies accordingly.

Entrepreneur A's journey also highlights the importance of sustainability in entrepreneurship. They were committed to making a positive impact on the environment and society. By incorporating sustainable practices into their business model, they attracted like-minded customers who valued ethical and eco-friendly products. They understood that sustainability is not just a trend but a long-term commitment for both the planet and their business's success.

Throughout their journey, Entrepreneur A faced challenges, setbacks, and doubts. However, their passion, resilience, and determination kept them going. They surrounded themselves with a supportive network of mentors, advisors, and like-minded individuals who provided guidance and encouragement along the way.

Becoming an entrepreneur, a social media entrepreneur, or a sustainable entrepreneur requires hard work, dedication, and a willingness to take risks. Entrepreneur A's story serves as a reminder that success is not achieved overnight but through continuous learning, adaptation, and perseverance.

As a young person interested in entrepreneurship, you have the power to break the mold and create your own path. By learning from entrepreneurs like Entrepreneur A, you can gain the inspiration and knowledge needed to turn your ideas into successful ventures. So, let their story guide you on your own journey from idea to success.

Entrepreneur B: Leveraging Social Media for Business Growth

In today's digital age, social media has become an essential tool for businesses to thrive and grow. It has revolutionized the way entrepreneurs connect with their target audience, market their products or services, and build a brand. In this subchapter, we will explore how young entrepreneurs can leverage social media to their advantage and achieve business success.

Social media platforms such as Facebook, Instagram, Twitter, and LinkedIn offer immense opportunities for aspiring entrepreneurs. With billions of active users, these platforms provide an extensive reach to a global audience. By creating engaging and relevant content, entrepreneurs can attract potential customers, generate leads, and increase conversions.

To become a social media entrepreneur, it is crucial to understand the power of storytelling. Young people have a unique advantage in this realm as they are well-versed in the language and culture of social media. By creating authentic and relatable content, entrepreneurs can build a loyal following and establish a strong online presence.

One of the key aspects of leveraging social media for business growth is understanding the target audience. By conducting thorough market research and analyzing social media analytics, entrepreneurs can gain insights into their customers' preferences, behaviors, and needs. This information can then be used to tailor content and marketing strategies, making them more effective and impactful.

Another important consideration for young entrepreneurs is using social media as a tool for sustainable entrepreneurship. Today's generation is increasingly concerned about social and environmental issues. By aligning their businesses with sustainable practices and communicating these values through social media, entrepreneurs can attract conscious consumers who are willing to support ethical and eco-friendly brands.

Moreover, social media platforms also provide opportunities for collaboration and networking. Entrepreneurs can connect with like-minded individuals, industry influencers, and potential business partners. By building mutually beneficial relationships, young entrepreneurs can gain valuable mentorship, access new markets, and even find investors.

In conclusion, social media has become an indispensable tool for young entrepreneurs looking to make their mark in the business world. By leveraging the power of social media, entrepreneurs can reach a wider audience, build a strong brand, and drive business growth. Understanding the target audience, storytelling, and incorporating sustainable practices are key elements for success in this digital landscape. So, if you aspire to become an entrepreneur, embrace social media, and unlock its limitless potential for your business.

Entrepreneur C: Creating a Sustainable Business Model

In the ever-changing landscape of entrepreneurship, creating a sustainable business model has become an essential aspect for young aspiring entrepreneurs. In this subchapter, we will explore the key elements of building a sustainable business model, with a focus on social media entrepreneurship and sustainable practices.

1. Understanding the Basics:
To become an entrepreneur, it is crucial to have a solid understanding of business fundamentals. This includes identifying a problem or need in the market, developing a solution, and finding a target audience. Building a sustainable business model involves integrating these basics with sustainable practices.

2. Embracing Social Media:
Social media has revolutionized the way we communicate and conduct business. Aspiring social media entrepreneurs should leverage these platforms to build their brand, reach their target audience, and create a sustainable business model. Utilize social media tools to engage with customers, build a loyal community, and implement effective marketing strategies.

3. Incorporating Sustainability:
In today's environmentally conscious world, sustainable entrepreneurship has gained immense popularity. To become a sustainable entrepreneur, consider incorporating eco-friendly practices into your business model. This could include using sustainable materials, reducing waste, and implementing energy-efficient solutions. Consumers are increasingly attracted to businesses that prioritize sustainability, making it a valuable aspect of your business model.

4. Balancing Purpose and Profit:
While profitability is important, sustainable entrepreneurs understand the significance of balancing purpose and profit. By aligning your business goals with a larger purpose, such as addressing a social or environmental issue, you can create a sustainable business model that attracts both customers and investors who share your values.

5. Collaborating for Impact:
To become a successful sustainable entrepreneur, collaboration is key. Seek out partnerships and collaborations with like-minded businesses, nonprofits, and organizations. By working together, you can amplify your impact, reach a wider audience, and create a more sustainable future.

In conclusion, becoming an entrepreneur is an exciting journey, and building a sustainable business model is essential for long-term success. By understanding the basics of entrepreneurship, embracing social media, incorporating sustainability, balancing purpose and profit, and collaborating for impact, young aspiring entrepreneurs can create a successful and sustainable business.

Entrepreneur D: Overcoming Age-related Challenges

In the journey of entrepreneurship, age should never be a barrier to pursuing your dreams. Many successful entrepreneurs have started their ventures at a young age, proving that with passion, determination, and the right mindset, you can overcome age-related challenges and achieve your goals. In this subchapter, we will explore how young entrepreneurs can overcome obstacles and thrive in various entrepreneurial niches, including social media and sustainability.

When it comes to starting a business, age should not define your abilities. Instead, focus on your strengths and unique perspectives. Being young often means having fresh ideas and a willingness to take risks that older entrepreneurs may shy away from. Embrace your youth and use it as an advantage in your entrepreneurial journey.

For those aspiring to become social media entrepreneurs, age can actually be an advantage. Growing up in the digital age, young people have an innate understanding of social media platforms and trends. Use your knowledge and passion for social media to create engaging content, build a strong online presence, and connect with your target audience. Remember, authenticity and consistency are key to building a successful social media brand.

Becoming a sustainable entrepreneur is another exciting niche that young people can explore. The world is increasingly conscious of environmental issues, and sustainable businesses are in high demand. As a young person, you can bring fresh ideas and innovative solutions to the table. Research and educate yourself on sustainable practices, such as eco-friendly packaging, renewable energy, or ethical sourcing. By aligning your business with sustainability, you can not only make a positive impact on the planet but also attract a growing customer base that values environmentally conscious products and services.

While age-related challenges may exist, they should not discourage young entrepreneurs. Surround yourself with a supportive network of mentors, peers, and fellow entrepreneurs who can guide and inspire you. Seek out networking opportunities, attend workshops, and participate in entrepreneurship programs specifically designed for young people.

Remember, entrepreneurship is a journey, and success does not happen overnight. Embrace failures as learning experiences and stay persistent in pursuing your goals. With the right mindset, skills, and support, you can overcome age-related challenges and become a successful entrepreneur in any niche you choose.

So, young entrepreneurs, don't let age hold you back. Embrace your youth, leverage your unique perspectives, and create a path that leads you to entrepreneurial success. The world needs your ideas, your passion, and your drive to make a difference. Start breaking the mold today!

Lessons Learned from Young Entrepreneurs' Journeys

In the world of entrepreneurship, age is no longer a barrier to success. Young people across the globe are breaking the mold and making their mark in various industries. Their journeys are filled with valuable lessons that can inspire and guide aspiring entrepreneurs. In this subchapter, we will explore the insights gained from the experiences of these young entrepreneurs, specifically focusing on how to become an entrepreneur, a social media entrepreneur, and a sustainable entrepreneur.

To become an entrepreneur, the first lesson is to embrace failure. Many successful young entrepreneurs faced numerous setbacks before achieving their goals. They learned to view failure as an opportunity for growth and were not deterred by initial rejections or obstacles. Developing resilience and persistence is key to overcoming challenges and finding success in the entrepreneurial world.

For those interested in becoming a social media entrepreneur, the lesson is to harness the power of digital platforms. Young entrepreneurs have recognized the potential of social media in reaching a large audience and building a brand. They have become skilled at leveraging platforms like Instagram, YouTube, and TikTok to create engaging content, connect with their target audience, and monetize their online presence. By understanding the algorithms and trends, young social media entrepreneurs have been able to build thriving businesses.

In the realm of sustainable entrepreneurship, the lesson is to prioritize purpose over profit. Young entrepreneurs have shown a strong commitment to creating businesses that not only generate revenue but also have a positive impact on society and the environment. They have embraced sustainability as a core value and integrated it into their business models. These entrepreneurs have successfully demonstrated that it is possible to build profitable ventures while also making a difference in the world.

In conclusion, the journeys of young entrepreneurs offer valuable lessons for aspiring entrepreneurs. They teach us the importance of resilience, embracing failure, leveraging social media, and prioritizing purpose over profit. Whether you dream of becoming a general entrepreneur, a social media entrepreneur, or a sustainable entrepreneur, these lessons will serve as a guiding light on your own entrepreneurial journey. So, take inspiration from these young trailblazers and forge your own path towards success.

Chapter 7: Resources and Tools for Young Entrepreneurs

Books, Blogs, and Podcasts on Entrepreneurship

In today's fast-paced and ever-changing world, entrepreneurship has become an attractive career path for young people seeking to make a difference and create their own opportunities. Fortunately, there is a wealth of knowledge and resources available to help aspiring entrepreneurs navigate the exciting and challenging journey of starting their own business. This subchapter aims to introduce young people to a variety of books, blogs, and podcasts that offer valuable insights and guidance on becoming an entrepreneur, specifically focusing on three niches: how to become an entrepreneur, how to become a social media entrepreneur, and how to become a sustainable entrepreneur.

1. How to Become an Entrepreneur:
- "The Lean Startup" by Eric Ries: This book provides a practical guide to building a successful startup by adopting a lean and iterative approach.
- "Zero to One" by Peter Thiel: Thiel shares his insights on building groundbreaking companies and the importance of innovation in creating a valuable business.
- "The $100 Startup" by Chris Guillebeau: This book showcases inspiring stories of entrepreneurs who started their businesses with minimal resources and offers practical tips for getting started.

2. How to Become a Social Media Entrepreneur:
- "Crushing It!" by Gary Vaynerchuk: Vaynerchuk delves into the power of social media platforms and provides strategies for leveraging them to build a personal brand and business.
- "Jab, Jab, Jab, Right Hook" by Gary Vaynerchuk: This book focuses on creating engaging content and mastering the art of storytelling to effectively market products or services on social media.
- "Social Media Marketing Workbook" by Jason McDonald: McDonald's guide offers step-by-step instructions on how to use different social media platforms to grow a business and reach a wider audience.

3. How to Become a Sustainable Entrepreneur:
- "The Clean Money Revolution" by Joel Solomon: Solomon explores the concept of "clean money" and how entrepreneurs can align their businesses with sustainable and ethical practices.
- "The Responsible Entrepreneur" by Carol Sanford: This book challenges traditional notions of entrepreneurship and emphasizes the importance of creating businesses that contribute positively to society and the environment.
- "Drawdown" edited by Paul Hawken: Hawken brings together a comprehensive collection of solutions for combating climate change and highlights how entrepreneurs can play a crucial role in implementing these solutions.

Remember, these are just a few examples among a vast array of resources available. Blogs like Entrepreneur, Forbes, and Inc. offer valuable articles and insights from successful entrepreneurs, while podcasts such as "The Tim Ferriss Show" and "How I Built This" provide in-depth interviews with industry leaders. By immersing themselves in these resources, young people can gain valuable knowledge, inspiration, and practical advice to embark on their entrepreneurial journey.

Online Courses and Training Programs

In today's digital age, the world is at our fingertips. The internet has revolutionized the way we learn, connect, and do business. As a young person with aspirations of becoming an entrepreneur, you have a wealth of resources available to you, including online courses and training programs that can provide you with the knowledge and skills needed to succeed in your chosen niche.

Whether you have a burning desire to start your own business, become a social media entrepreneur, or make a positive impact on the world as a sustainable entrepreneur, there is an online course or training program tailored to your specific needs and interests.

To become an entrepreneur, it is crucial to have a solid foundation of business knowledge. Online courses can offer you a comprehensive overview of various aspects of entrepreneurship, such as business planning, marketing, finance, and management. These courses often include interactive modules, case studies, and real-world examples that will help you understand the intricacies of starting and running a successful business.

If your passion lies in social media entrepreneurship, online courses can equip you with the skills to navigate the ever-changing landscape of social media platforms. You will learn how to create engaging content, build a loyal following, and monetize your online presence. These courses often provide insights from successful social media entrepreneurs who have built thriving businesses through their online platforms.

For those interested in making a positive impact on the environment and society, sustainable entrepreneurship is a compelling niche to explore. Online training programs can teach you how to develop sustainable business models, incorporate eco-friendly practices, and create products or services that contribute to a more sustainable future. These programs often highlight successful sustainable entrepreneurs who have found innovative solutions to pressing global issues.

Online courses and training programs offer flexibility and convenience, allowing you to learn at your own pace and fit your studies around your existing commitments. They also provide the opportunity to connect with like-minded individuals from around the world, building a network of contacts that can support and inspire you on your entrepreneurial journey.

So, if you are a young person with dreams of becoming an entrepreneur, don't underestimate the power of online courses and training programs. They can provide you with the knowledge, skills, and inspiration needed to break the mold and create your own path in the business world. Embrace the opportunities that the digital age brings and unlock your full potential as an aspiring entrepreneur.

Networking Opportunities and Events

In the world of entrepreneurship, networking is key. Building relationships, making connections, and expanding your professional network can open up a world of opportunities for young entrepreneurs. Whether you aspire to become a traditional entrepreneur, a social media entrepreneur, or a sustainable entrepreneur, attending networking events and taking advantage of networking opportunities is crucial to your success.

Networking events provide a platform for like-minded individuals to come together, exchange ideas, and form valuable connections. These events can range from industry-specific conferences and trade shows to small meetups and workshops. By attending these events, you not only get the chance to learn from established entrepreneurs but also meet potential mentors, partners, or even investors.

For those interested in becoming a traditional entrepreneur, networking events focused on business development or entrepreneurship can be particularly beneficial. These events often feature successful entrepreneurs who share their stories, insights, and expertise. They provide an excellent opportunity to learn from their experiences, ask questions, and gain valuable advice. Additionally, you can connect with other aspiring entrepreneurs who may become your future collaborators or even co-founders.

If your entrepreneurial ambitions lean towards the realm of social media, attending networking events that specifically cater to this niche is essential. These events may focus on topics like social media marketing, influencer partnerships, or content creation. By participating in these events, you can learn from industry experts, discover current trends, and build relationships with other social media entrepreneurs. These connections can lead to collaborations, cross-promotions, and increased visibility for your brand.

For those interested in sustainable entrepreneurship, networking events centered around sustainability, environmental conservation, or social impact can be invaluable. These events gather individuals who are passionate about creating businesses that prioritize the planet and society. Attending such events can help you connect with sustainable entrepreneurs, environmental experts, and socially responsible investors. These connections can provide mentorship, guidance, and potential funding for your sustainable business ideas.

In conclusion, networking opportunities and events are critical for young entrepreneurs, regardless of the specific niche they aspire to enter. By attending these events, you can learn from industry experts, meet potential mentors or partners, and build a strong professional network. Whether you want to become a traditional entrepreneur, a social media entrepreneur, or a sustainable entrepreneur, networking events offer a valuable platform to connect, learn, and grow. So, don't miss out on these opportunities and make the most out of the networking events available to you!

Funding and Support Organizations

As a young person with dreams of becoming an entrepreneur, you may find the journey daunting, especially when it comes to securing the necessary funds to get your business off the ground. However, fear not! There are numerous funding and support organizations available to help young entrepreneurs like you turn their ideas into reality.

1. Start with traditional funding options: Depending on your business idea, you may be eligible for grants, loans, or venture capital from traditional funding sources. Research local and national government programs, banks, and angel investor networks to explore these possibilities.

2. Seek out startup incubators and accelerators: These organizations are specifically designed to support young entrepreneurs in refining their ideas, developing business plans, and connecting with potential investors. Many offer mentorship, office space, and access to a network of experienced professionals.

3. Explore crowdfunding platforms: Crowdfunding has become a popular way for entrepreneurs to raise capital by leveraging their social networks. Platforms such as Kickstarter, Indiegogo, and GoFundMe allow you to showcase your business idea and attract financial support from individuals interested in your product or service.

4. Connect with venture philanthropy organizations: If your entrepreneurial aspirations are focused on making a positive social impact, venture philanthropy organizations can provide both funding and support. These organizations seek out business ideas that align with their mission and offer financial assistance along with guidance on developing sustainable and socially conscious businesses.

5. Look into specific industry grants and competitions: Many industries have their own funding opportunities for young entrepreneurs. Whether you're interested in technology, agriculture, or fashion, there are likely grants and competitions specifically tailored to your niche. These opportunities not only provide financial support but also give you a chance to gain exposure and build your network.

Remember, funding is just one piece of the puzzle. Alongside financial support, seek out organizations that offer mentorship and guidance. Surrounding yourself with experienced individuals who can offer advice and share their own entrepreneurial journeys will be invaluable to your success.

Becoming an entrepreneur, especially in the realms of social media or sustainability, requires dedication, passion, and a strong support system. By tapping into the resources provided by funding and support organizations, you can overcome financial barriers and set yourself up for a successful entrepreneurial journey. Embrace the opportunities available to you, and let your innovative ideas shape the future of business.

Tools and Software for Business Management

In today's digital age, technology plays a crucial role in every aspect of our lives, including business management. Whether you aspire to become an entrepreneur, a social media entrepreneur, or a sustainable entrepreneur, having the right tools and software at your disposal can make all the difference in achieving success. In this subchapter, we will explore some essential tools and software that can streamline your business operations and help you stay ahead of the game.

1. Project Management Tools: As an entrepreneur, you will often find yourself juggling multiple projects simultaneously. Project management tools like Trello, Asana, or Monday.com can assist you in organizing tasks, setting deadlines, assigning responsibilities, and tracking progress. These tools ensure that nothing falls through the cracks and help you stay on top of your game.

2. Customer Relationship Management (CRM) Software: Building and maintaining strong relationships with your customers is vital for any business. CRM software, such as Salesforce or HubSpot, can help you manage customer interactions, track sales, and analyze customer data. These tools enable you to provide personalized experiences and nurture long-term relationships with your clientele.

3. Accounting and Bookkeeping Software: Managing finances is a critical aspect of entrepreneurship. Tools like QuickBooks or Xero can simplify your bookkeeping tasks, track expenses and revenue, generate financial reports, and even assist with invoicing and payroll. These software solutions take the hassle out of financial management, allowing you to focus on growing your business.

4. Social Media Management Tools: For those interested in becoming social media entrepreneurs, tools like Hootsuite or Buffer can be game-changers. These platforms allow you to schedule and manage your social media posts across multiple platforms, analyze engagement metrics, and monitor your brand's online presence. With these tools, you can effectively reach and engage with your target audience, driving traffic and sales to your business.

5. Sustainability Tracking Tools: If your goal is to become a sustainable entrepreneur, there are various tools available that can help you measure and track your environmental impact. Platforms like Ecologi or Good On You provide insights into carbon emissions, ethical sourcing, and sustainable practices. By utilizing these tools, you can make informed decisions and showcase your commitment to sustainability to attract conscious consumers.

Remember, as a young entrepreneur, it's essential to stay updated with the latest tools and software that can enhance your business management skills. Embracing technology and leveraging these resources will not only make your life easier but also give you a competitive edge in the ever-evolving business landscape. So, equip yourself with these tools, explore their features, and take your entrepreneurial journey to new heights.

Mentorship Programs and Platforms

In today's fast-paced and ever-evolving world, mentorship has become an invaluable resource for young people aspiring to become entrepreneurs. Mentors provide guidance, support, and a wealth of knowledge that can help navigate the complex journey of entrepreneurship. Fortunately, there are numerous mentorship programs and platforms available that cater to the specific needs and interests of aspiring entrepreneurs, including those interested in social media and sustainable entrepreneurship.

One of the most important steps in becoming an entrepreneur is finding the right mentor. Mentorship programs and platforms offer a structured and supportive environment for young individuals to connect with experienced entrepreneurs who have already walked the path they aspire to take. These mentors can provide invaluable insights into the challenges and opportunities that lie ahead, offering practical advice and guidance based on their own experiences.

For those interested in becoming a social media entrepreneur, mentorship programs and platforms can be particularly beneficial. Social media platforms have revolutionized the way businesses connect with their target audience, making it an attractive avenue for young entrepreneurs. Mentorship programs tailored to social media entrepreneurship can provide guidance on building a personal brand, creating engaging content, and leveraging social media platforms to drive business growth. Mentors who have successfully built their own social media empires can offer firsthand knowledge and expertise, helping young entrepreneurs navigate the ever-changing landscape of social media marketing.

Similarly, sustainable entrepreneurship has gained traction in recent years, as young people are increasingly concerned about the environment and social impact. Mentorship programs and platforms focusing on sustainable entrepreneurship can provide guidance on developing businesses that prioritize sustainability, ethical practices, and positive social impact. Mentors in this field can offer insights into creating environmentally-friendly products or services, building partnerships with socially-responsible organizations, and developing marketing strategies that resonate with conscious consumers.

In conclusion, mentorship programs and platforms play a crucial role in supporting young people who aspire to become entrepreneurs. Whether one's interest lies in general entrepreneurship, social media entrepreneurship, or sustainable entrepreneurship, these programs and platforms offer access to experienced mentors who can provide guidance, advice, and inspiration. By connecting with mentors who have successfully navigated the entrepreneurial journey, young individuals can gain the necessary tools and confidence to break the mold and pursue their entrepreneurial dreams.

Co-working Spaces and Incubators

In recent years, the entrepreneurial landscape has seen an exciting development with the rise of co-working spaces and incubators. These innovative workspaces have become a hub for aspiring entrepreneurs, providing them with an environment that fosters creativity, collaboration, and growth. Whether you aspire to become a traditional entrepreneur, a social media entrepreneur, or a sustainable entrepreneur, these spaces can play a pivotal role in your journey towards success.

Co-working spaces are shared workspaces that bring together individuals from various industries and backgrounds. They offer a flexible and affordable alternative to traditional offices, making them particularly appealing to young entrepreneurs who may not have the resources to rent their own space. These spaces provide access to amenities such as high-speed internet, meeting rooms, and communal areas, creating an environment that encourages networking and collaboration. By working alongside like-minded individuals, you can tap into a valuable network of potential mentors, partners, and clients.

Incubators, on the other hand, take co-working spaces to the next level by providing additional support and resources specifically tailored to early-stage startups. These programs offer mentorship, access to funding, and educational workshops to help entrepreneurs refine their business ideas and accelerate their growth. Incubators often have a specific focus, such as technology, social impact, or sustainability, making them an excellent choice for those interested in niche entrepreneurial ventures.

For young people looking to become entrepreneurs, co-working spaces and incubators offer numerous advantages. Firstly, they provide a supportive community of like-minded individuals who understand the challenges and triumphs of starting a business. This network can offer invaluable advice, feedback, and inspiration throughout your entrepreneurial journey. Additionally, the collaborative environment of these spaces fosters innovation and creativity, allowing you to bounce ideas off others and gain fresh perspectives on your business concept.

If you aspire to become a social media entrepreneur, co-working spaces and incubators can be particularly beneficial. They offer access to cutting-edge technology, such as state-of-the-art photo and video equipment, editing software, and social media analytics tools. Moreover, the diverse community within these spaces can help you stay updated on the latest trends and strategies in the ever-evolving world of social media.

For those interested in sustainable entrepreneurship, co-working spaces and incubators can provide a platform to connect with like-minded individuals who share your passion for creating positive environmental and social impact. These spaces often host events and workshops focusing on sustainability, allowing you to deepen your knowledge and expand your network within the sustainable business community.

In conclusion, co-working spaces and incubators have revolutionized the way entrepreneurs work and collaborate. Regardless of your entrepreneurial niche, these spaces offer a supportive community, access to resources, and opportunities for growth and learning. By immersing yourself in a co-working space or joining an incubator program, you can kickstart your entrepreneurial journey and increase your chances of success.

Tips for Constant Learning and Self-Improvement

In today's rapidly changing world, constant learning and self-improvement are crucial for anyone looking to become an entrepreneur. Whether you aspire to be a traditional entrepreneur, a social media entrepreneur, or a sustainable entrepreneur, the path to success begins with a commitment to personal growth and a hunger for knowledge. In this subchapter, we will explore some valuable tips that will help you on your journey towards becoming a successful entrepreneur.

1. Embrace a Growth Mindset: Adopting a growth mindset is essential for continuous learning and self-improvement. Understand that your abilities and intelligence can be developed through dedication and hard work. Embrace challenges, seek out feedback, and view failures as opportunities to learn and grow.

2. Never Stop Learning: As an entrepreneur, it is vital to stay updated with the latest industry trends, technologies, and business practices. Make a habit of reading books, attending seminars, and participating in online courses to broaden your knowledge base. Seek mentors who can guide you and provide valuable insights from their own experiences.

3. Be Curious and Ask Questions: Curiosity is the fuel that drives innovation. Develop a natural curiosity about the world around you and ask questions. Always remain curious about various aspects of entrepreneurship, from marketing strategies to sustainable business practices. Curiosity will keep you ahead of the game and enable you to adapt to new challenges and opportunities.

4. Network and Collaborate: Surround yourself with like-minded individuals who share your passion for entrepreneurship. Attend industry events, join entrepreneurial communities, and actively engage with professionals in your field. Collaboration with others will not only help you learn from their experiences but also open doors to potential partnerships and business opportunities.

5. Emphasize Personal Growth: Self-improvement goes beyond just acquiring business skills. Focus on personal growth as well by cultivating habits that enhance your well-being, such as practicing mindfulness, maintaining a healthy lifestyle, and prioritizing work-life balance. Remember that a healthy mind and body are essential for long-term success.

6. Embrace Failure and Learn from Mistakes: Failure is an inevitable part of the entrepreneurial journey. Instead of being discouraged by setbacks, embrace them as valuable learning opportunities. Analise your mistakes, identify areas for improvement, and adapt your strategies accordingly. Remember, every successful entrepreneur has faced failures but used them as stepping stones to success.

Constant learning and self-improvement are the keys to becoming a successful entrepreneur. By embracing a growth mindset, staying curious, networking, and learning from failures, you will position yourself for success in whichever entrepreneurial niche you choose. Remember, the journey towards entrepreneurship is a continuous process, so keep pushing yourself, stay hungry for knowledge, and never stop striving for excellence.

Chapter 8: Conclusion and Final Thoughts

Recap of Key Lessons and Takeaways

As we come to the end of our journey through the book "Breaking the Mold: A Young Person's Guide to Entrepreneurship," it is essential to recap the key lessons and takeaways that can empower you on your path to becoming a successful entrepreneur. Whether you aspire to start your own business, become a social media entrepreneur, or focus on sustainable entrepreneurship, these lessons are applicable to all young people looking to embark on this exciting journey.

Lesson 1: Passion and Purpose
One of the fundamental lessons we've learned is the importance of finding your passion and aligning it with a purpose. Identifying what truly drives you will not only give your entrepreneurial journey meaning but also provide the motivation and resilience needed to overcome challenges.

Lesson 2: The Power of Innovation
Entrepreneurship thrives on innovation. Embrace your creativity and think outside the box to develop unique solutions to problems. Emphasize the importance of continuous learning and adaptability to stay ahead in a rapidly evolving business landscape.

Lesson 3: Building a Strong Network

Networking is a crucial aspect of entrepreneurship. Surround yourself with like-minded individuals who can provide mentorship, guidance, and support. Attend workshops, conferences, and join entrepreneurial communities to expand your network and gain valuable insights from experts.

Lesson 4: Embracing Failure and Resilience

Failure is an inevitable part of the entrepreneurial journey. Instead of being discouraged, see it as an opportunity to learn, grow, and improve. Developing resilience will enable you to bounce back stronger and more determined to succeed.

Lesson 5: Adapting to the Digital Age

In today's digital era, it is vital to harness the power of technology and social media. If you are interested in becoming a social media entrepreneur, focus on building a strong online presence, understanding your target audience, and leveraging various platforms to promote your business or brand effectively.

Lesson 6: Sustainable Entrepreneurship

With the growing focus on environmental and social responsibility, sustainable entrepreneurship has become increasingly important. Consider the impact of your business on the environment and society, and explore ways to incorporate sustainable practices into your operations.

By internalizing these key lessons, you are well on your way to becoming a successful entrepreneur, regardless of your chosen niche. Remember, entrepreneurship is a journey, and it requires dedication, perseverance, and continuous learning. As a young person, you have the power to break the mold and create your path to success. So, go forth with confidence, embrace your entrepreneurial spirit, and make a positive impact on the world through your ventures. Good luck!

Encouragement to Pursue Entrepreneurship

Introduction:
In today's rapidly evolving world, the concept of traditional career paths is being challenged by the vast opportunities presented by entrepreneurship. As a young person, you have the power to break free from the mold and forge your own path towards success. This subchapter aims to inspire and encourage you to pursue entrepreneurship, focusing on three distinct niches: how to become an entrepreneur, how to become a social media entrepreneur, and how to become a sustainable entrepreneur.

Embracing the Journey of Breaking the Mold

In the pursuit of success and fulfillment, many young people find themselves yearning for something different, something beyond the confines of traditional paths. This subchapter, "Embracing the Journey of Breaking the Mold," from the book "Breaking the Mold: A Young Person's Guide to Entrepreneurship," aims to inspire and guide young individuals who are eager to explore the world of entrepreneurship.

Becoming an entrepreneur is not just about starting a business; it is a mindset, a way of thinking, and a commitment to challenging the status quo. In this subchapter, we will delve into the transformative journey of breaking the mold, encouraging young people to embrace their unique ideas and pave their own paths towards success.

Entrepreneurship is an all-encompassing adventure that requires passion, dedication, and resilience. We will explore the essential steps to becoming an entrepreneur, starting with identifying your passions and interests, honing your skills, and embracing failure as a stepping stone to success. By learning from the experiences of successful entrepreneurs, you will gain valuable insights and strategies to overcome obstacles and navigate the ever-changing landscape of entrepreneurship.

For those interested in becoming a social media entrepreneur, we will explore the power of digital platforms in today's interconnected world. From creating compelling content to building an online brand and engaging with your audience, we will provide practical tips and techniques to establish your presence and make a meaningful impact through social media. Learn how to leverage the immense potential of Instagram, YouTube, TikTok, or any other platform to turn your passion into a thriving business.

Furthermore, we cannot ignore the urgent need for sustainable entrepreneurship. As young people, we have a responsibility to address pressing environmental and social challenges. This subchapter will inspire and equip young entrepreneurs to build sustainable businesses that prioritize social and environmental impact. You will discover innovative approaches to create businesses that promote eco-friendly practices, address social inequalities, and contribute to a more sustainable future.

"Embracing the Journey of Breaking the Mold" is a call to action for young people who refuse to settle for conventional paths and aspire to make a difference. By exploring the realms of entrepreneurship, social media, and sustainability, this subchapter will empower you to embrace your unique journey, break the mold, and create a fulfilling and impactful career. Remember, the future is yours to shape, and the possibilities are limitless when you dare to dream and take that courageous leap into the world of entrepreneurship.

Final Words of Inspiration for Young Entrepreneurs

Congratulations on embarking on the journey of entrepreneurship! As a young person with a passion for creating your own path, you possess the power to shape your future and make a positive impact on the world. This final chapter is dedicated to providing you with some inspiring words of wisdom to fuel your entrepreneurial spirit and guide you along the way.

In conclusion, becoming an entrepreneur is an exciting journey filled with challenges and rewards. Embrace your passion, believe in yourself, and never stop learning and growing. Whether you choose to become a traditional entrepreneur, a social media entrepreneur, or a sustainable entrepreneur, remember that the path to success is paved with determination, resilience, and a desire to make a difference. Now, go out there and break the mold! The world is waiting for your entrepreneurial spirit to shine.